Stories by Meir Blinkin

Stories by Meir Blinkin

Translated from the Yiddish by Max Rosenfeld

With an Introduction by Ruth R. Wisse

The SUNY Series in Modern Jewish Literature and Culture

Sarah Blacher Cohen, Editor

State University of New York Press   Albany

Published by State University of New York Press, Albany
© 1984 State University of New York   All rights reserved
Printed in the United States of America
No part of this book may be used or reproduced in any
manner whatsoever without written permission except
in the case of brief quotations embodied in critical ar-
ticles and reviews.
For information, address State University of New York
Press, State University Plaza, Albany, N.Y., 12246

Library of Congress Cataloging in Publication Data
Blinkin, Meir, 1879–1915.
Stories.
1. Blinkin, Meir, 1879–1915—Translations, English.
I. Rosenfeld, Max, 1913–   II. Title.
PJ5129.B5765A26   1984   839'.0933   83-15564
ISBN 0-87395-818-7

Contents

Introduction

BY RUTH R. WISSE

THIS IS THE STORY of an interrupted literary career. Meir Blinken* was born in 1879, twenty years after the great Yiddish writer Sholem Aleichem, in the same small town of Pereyeslav, within the Jewish Pale of Settlement. He recalled his birthplace as a poor, insulated community, "surrounded by high thick woods, as though designed to prevent strangers from prying." While he was still a boy, his parents moved with him to Kiev, the capital of the Ukraine, evidently seeking better economic opportunities for themselves and their children. As a major city, Kiev was outside the limits of Jewish settlement, except for that tiny minority with capital or skills that were considered essential. The parents of Meir Blinken were probably among the many hundreds of Jews who were driven by poverty to try their luck in the larger city despite the fugitive existence to which this condemned them.

Blinken was educated in a Talmud Torah, a community-supported Jewish primary school, and then at the Kiev Trade School, where he received a secular education. He began the study of medicine, but because of the need for a residence permit, granted only to those engaged in useful trade, he was also apprenticed to a cabinetmaker to learn the skills of carpentry.

---

* Meir Blinkin's name was spelled Blinkin, but the immigration authorities changed the second "i" to an "e" so that the official records were always spelled Blinken. I use the American authorities' version ending in "ken."

(Sholem Aleichem's wife, Olga, had become a dentist in order to secure for her family the residence permit that was otherwise denied them.) It may be assumed that like most young Jews with intellectual inclinations, Blinken was caught up by the liberal opposition to the Czar, and sympathized with the growing revolutionary movement. But he had married young and his immediate concern was for elemental safety. The combination of native anti-Semitism and czarist agitation against the Jews resulted in a wave of pogroms throughout the Ukraine between 1902 and 1905, forcing thousands of Jews to flee for their lives. Blinken temporarily left his wife and two sons and set out for America. He arrived in New York in 1904, at the age of twenty-five, one of some 105,000 Jews to reach America that year.

By the time of Blinken's arrival, the Lower East Side of Manhattan was the most densely populated area on the globe, thanks to the unprecedented influx of new immigrants. Newcomers from similar backgrounds preferred to cluster together so as to provide one another with at least some buttressing familiarity on this new continent. The Jews, too, formed their own neighborhoods, dotted with tiny synagogues and *landsmanschaften,* fraternal associations of people from the same Old Country locales. Although it was often much harder to make a living than they had hoped, the immigrants were not deceived in their other expectations of American freedom, particularly the right to free expression. Whereas newspapers, theaters, publication, and assembly had been checked by strict censorship in Russia, anyone with imagination and a line of credit could in the new country mount almost any form of entertainment, instruction, or persuasion. Not surprisingly, the Jewish immigrants took immediate advantage of this possibility for self-expression to create a whole new cultural presence.

Meir Blinken had begun to write while he was still a student of medicine in Kiev. Upon landing in New York, he met up with dozens of other novices like himself, whose literary ambition was not inhibited in the least by their lack of formal training. Yiddish, the vernacular of the great majority of Jewish immigrants, indeed, of world Jewry, was the natural me-

dium of Jewish culture both in Russia and in America. As a
budding Yiddish writer, Blinken was confronted by endless
opportunity in the form of several daily Yiddish newspapers,
sprouting new magazines and literary societies, all looking for
material and fellow readers. There were special restaurants
frequented by the established editors and authors, and excitement enough for a young man who wanted to establish himself as a writer.

One of the remarkable features of this spirited cultural
flowering among the immigrant Jews on the Lower East Side
at the beginning of this century was the gap between their
proletarian existence and their high artistic aspirations. Since
most of the aspiring writers arrived in the new country without trade or profession, they had to earn their living as ordinary workers or go hungry trying to sell their poems and
stories for the going rate of a few dollars per item. After bringing over his family from Kiev, Blinken had to support them
all, which could not be done, even by the most accomplished
writers, on the basis of publication alone. His craft gave him
something of an advantage over those of his fellow artists
who had to take employment in the local factories or as window washers, paperhangers, and painters. Blinken worked at
carpentry, then opened an office on East Broadway, in the
heart of the Yiddish publishing district, and offered his services as a masseur, evidently on the basis of skills he had ac-
quired while at medical school in Kiev. Despite his difficult
circumstances, and an unsettled family life, he published over
fifty items within a decade of his arrival.

Blinken's awareness of the discrepancy between the material, menial requirements of subsistence and his own cultural needs is the subject of one of his first pieces, a feuilleton
with a strong autobiographical strain, that appeared in the socialist weekly *Der Arbeter* (The Worker). In it the narrator describes a chance encounter, on January 10, 1906, on East 80th
Street, with a young man he had known in Kiev who once
borrowed some books from him. The two Kiev acquaintances
discuss their experiences since their arrival in America. While
the narrator longs to be back in Russia, and speaks nostalgi-
cally of his past, his friend is full of praise for the new home:

He said he was in love with America. He feels that here, if
you but have the will, you can achieve everything you
want. If you but keep your eyes open, your nose off the
ground, thrust forward with elbows pushing left and right,
you can get very far.

The narrator is impressed by this brash philosophy. He sus-
pects that his friend must have made a bundle for himself in
real estate or law. It turns out, however, that this buoyancy is
based on nothing more than the job the friend has found walking a lawyer's dog twice a day for five dollars a week. Like
most of his young colleagues, Blinken mocked the emphasis
on economic "security" that was so prevalent in the immigrant community, recognizing how comically out of step his
own cultural quest seemed to be with the general spirit of the
Jewish street.

    The youthful American Yiddish literature of which Blin-
ken was becoming a part stood in a unique relation to both its
own past and to the surrounding culture. By the beginning of
the century the first generations of modern Yiddish writers
had already laid down a broad and deep foundation for the literature. Writers like Shloime Ettinger, I. I. Linetski, Yakov
Dineson, and the three giants of Yiddish fiction—Mendele
Mocher Sforim (Sholem Yakov Abramovitch), Sholem Aleichem (Sholem Rabinovitch), and I. L. Peretz—had experi-
mented successfully with various literary genres and levels of
language to see what could and could not be fruitfully at-
tempted in the East European Jewish vernacular. The writers
of Blinken's generation thus inherited the beginnings of a literary "tradition" against which they were now free to test
their own powers. To be sure, the young American writers
called themselves cultural orphans, and liked to flaunt their
rebellion against the conventions of their predecessors, but
this very rebelliousness confirmed their debt.

    At the same time, the experiment was still very young,
especially when Yiddish was compared with other Western
literatures. All Yiddish writers were familiar with at least one

or two or more other languages, and followed avidly the latest artistic movements of Europe and America. Every young writer felt the challenge of attempting in Yiddish some artistic innovation, although the better writers understood how much depended on their indigenous culture and on the range of their own linguistic instrument. At least part of the spirit of renaissance derived from the collective desire to make Yiddish literature responsive to the new artistic trends, and thus "catch up" with the literary achievements of other Western cultures.

But perhaps the most important stimulus to the artistic flowering was the situation of these Jewish writers as part of an extraordinarily rapid transition from a firmly traditional way of life to an uprooted mass of individuals, grasping for new directions. In "Dr. Machover," Blinken traces the transformation of an Orthodox Jewish child—born at a time when there were only "orthodox" Jewish children—into a freethinking man of science. The young boy's crisis of faith is typically sudden: one day he is a devout scholar of the Talmud; the next, he finds an inscription warning him that "all you learn is false. There is no God, there is no hell." This decisively undermines his belief and the life based upon it. Since the life-style of the Jews, involving almost every aspect of their daily routine, was bound up with the faith in which they were raised, its collapse meant a radical—and, in Blinken's view, disastrous—break with the past. Thus, Dr. Machover, like most of Blinken's generation, must find a new professional and philosophic sphere of identification. Machover's inability to find a satisfactory alternative to the religious certainty of his youth reflects the author's own dissatisfaction with some of the kinds of bargains Jews made with modernity.

The geographic upheaval for those who came to America necessitated an even more profound reorientation. In this new and unknown territory, so different from the landscape of Eastern Europe, there was a great need for new guides and interpreters, and much as the early explorers had charted the rivers and mountains, the writers and intellectuals within the Jewish milieu were expected to provide solid cultural and social guidelines for the evolving community. The writers felt

that they were part of a movement considerably larger than
the individual, requiring something of a consolidated effort,
and they banded together in literary clubs, publication com-
mittees, and every kind of artistic group.

The largest of these, a loose association of poets and writers who declared themselves to be striking out in new directions, was dubbed, simply, *di yugnt* (youth), and its adherents,
di yunge (the young), as if in acknowledgment that America
was now the home of a fresh literary generation. Among the
writers associated with this movement, many would rise to
great prominence: Mani Leib (Brahinsky, 1884–1953), Moishe
Leib Halpern (1886–1932), Zishe Landau (1889–1937), Joseph
Opatoshu (1886–1954), Isaac Raboy (1885–1944), Joseph Rol-
nik (1879–1955), David Ignatoff (1895–1954), I. I. Schwartz
(1885–1971), and H. Leivick (Leivick Halpern, 1888–1962). In
the years before World War I, the heyday of this movement,
Meir Blinken was one of the most promising prose writers in
its ranks, recognized for his distinctive subject matter and
style.

Blinken's literary development, beginning with the publication of his earliest stories, is characteristic of the progress
of the *yunge*. His first efforts were filled with descriptive de-
tail of the constricting, reductive effects of poverty and ignorance. In the manner of naturalistic fiction, his short stories
conveyed the accusation of social oppression, and its characters—orphans, the unemployed, hungry mothers and in-
fants—were recognizable as society's victims. During this
period, 1906–10, the conditions of most immigrants were
still wretched, and Blinken's descriptions of the overcrowded
tenement flats and sweatshop conditions have about them the
authenticity of hard-won experience.

Nevertheless, even in these earliest stories, we see the
author's interest veering away from social scrutiny to the
penetration of psychological and emotional states. He takes
over from his literary elders, whose sketches filled the local
press, their preoccupation with the poor and the suffering, but
without trying to create pathos or sentimentality. Instead,
Blinken uses the atmosphere of poverty as a background, and
concentrates on the nuances of human interaction, the moods

of characters under stress, especially within family life. One of his favorite subjects is the attraction of a married woman to a close friend or relative of the husband's, since the development of this situation creates a strained period of shifting emotions, the very kind of tension that Blinken chooses as his artistic own. The shift of focus from social problems to analysis of mood was the basis of the rebellion that the *yunge* mounted against their elders, and Blinken typifies their approach.

"Family Life: A Chapter," the earliest of Blinken's works to be included in this collection, shows a deliberately shocking liaison between a wife and her brother-in-law who is also her secret lover and the father of her youngest child. It is clear that the youthful author revels a little in the sensationalism of his subject, and in the introduction of such racy material to readers who had been raised on the strict standards of sexual purity that form a crucial part of Jewish law. Yet it is also evident that Blinken's deeper interest lies in describing not so much the liaison itself as the curious mixture of domesticity and licentiousness that binds the lovers. While the sexual passion of the lovers is heightened, if not actually inspired, by the forbidden nature of their union (which thrives within the very bosom of the two related families), their close family ties and burdensome proximity also intrude on their passion, so that the love affair becomes a reflection of their domestic unhappiness rather than an alternative to it. In several such stories of marital infidelity Blinken chooses the perspective of the woman, who is looking for a happier life, but traps herself instead in a repetition of her former misery.

Blinken realized that his subject matter derived from the sentimental romance. He even drew attention to the banality of his device by calling one of his stories, in which a woman falls in love with her husband's partner, "The Old, Old Song." Nonetheless, he continued to put the cliché of the romantic triangle to new use, granting the premise of the "old" plot in order to explore the modulation of feeling of his characters. "Card Game," published separately as a novella in 1914, was his most fully developed treatment of this theme, and it shows the range of Blinken's talent. Here the setting is a middle-class household rather than the tenement. Moyshe, the wealthy husband, has rescued his younger wife, Fanya, from her drudgery in a sweatshop, and thus seems to stand in absolute contrast to Meylekh, the husband in "Family Life: A Chapter," who could not provide even the bare necessities for his wife, Fradl.

The similarity in the names of the couple, however, alerts us to the underlying similarity of their union, which the improved conditions of their economic life have hardly changed. If poverty was the problem in the earlier story, wealth becomes the problem in this later one: Fanya has nothing to do all day and becomes the prey of fantasies, sexual cravings, and of women with far greater experience at realizing and satisfying them.

As he describes this atmosphere of leisure, the author also proceeds at a more leisurely narrative pace: he sketches in something of the surrounding society; the card-playing women who in teaching Fanya the various games also initiate her into the game of duplicitous sex of which card playing is here symbolic; and the men who are now thoroughly steeped in material concerns, and lack any other criterion of satisfaction. The transformation of Fanya from the innocent young bride into the deceitful romantic housewife suggests the desperation of boredom, the onset of moral decay that threatens the immigrant community as it works its way up the socioeconomic ladder.

We can see from contemporary criticism that several qualities of Blinken's writing were considered particularly innovative. He was singled out for his psychological observation. The *yunge* were fascinated by the problem of mood in literature, by which they meant the nuances of personal feeling as opposed to the concern for social fabric. Blinken's fiction was filled with studies of self-absorption, especially on the part of women who turn inward in various forms of recoil from their surroundings.

The Yiddish humor magazines, which were popular among the immigrant readers, are an unusually lively source of information about Blinken's work and its reception. The humor magazines like *Der Kibitzer* and *Der Groyser Kundes* (The Big Stick) carried many lampoons of contemporary literature, particularly of the writers who were also contributors, as Meir Blinken was. At one point he wrote a series of episodes describing the attempts of a writer to place his work in the various Yiddish periodicals and newspapers of the day. Each episode was a parody of the editorial policy of a different political figure: Abraham Cahan, editor of the *Jewish Daily Forward*; David Pinski, prominent writer and editor of the socialist *Arbeter*; Dr. Nahum Syrkin, editor of the Zionist *Folk*; and so on.

In the pages of these magazines there are many barbed references to Blinken's latest publications, never flattering, but sufficiently piquant to attract attention to the works they mocked, and in the nature of cartoons, to their most prominent features. Blinken's "Card Game," for example, was the subject of a "review" by the best of the humorists, Moishe Nadir, who offers a synopsis of the story and then complains:

> That Blinken has an eye—that we know. We will go further and grant that he has *two* eyes. But what does he do with them? . . . I ask you: Mister Blinken, where have you seen the Jewish woman who plays poker, lets herself be pinched, and "presses your head to her bosom?" In fact, we are interested in finding out where this kind of woman lives and where we could get in touch with her. Eh? Really—give us her address!

This is Nadir's way of saying that Blinken's depiction of Mrs. Resnick and the circle of card players that ensnares the young Fanya was quite daring for its time. Yiddish literature had not long before begun to treat the Jewish underworld and the coarser segments of Jewish society, but Blinken's concentration of females in this milieu was new, as was his interest in abnormal female psychology ("The Mysterious Secret").

Nadir's mockery also draws attention to a stylistic quality of Blinken's writing, one that cannot come across in translation but that impressed itself as a novelty upon contemporary readers. He notes the appendix of English terms that followed the story "Card Game":

> From this appendix it appears that Blinken had his head
> full of philology . . . and that he commands enough En-
> glish to be able to chat with the coal man and when nec-
> essary even to complain about the janitor.

When he was writing about the immigrants' acquiring new
wealth, Blinken did indeed try to capture their speech, which
was riddled with Anglicisms and malapropisms. Nadir's allu-
sion to Blinken's use of English is one of several such jibes
that appear over the years, indicating just how fresh a device
this seemed.

As a young writer in a fairly young literature, Blinken was
obviously influenced by the work of his predecessors, but one
can also see signs of his own influence on some of his contemporaries. The story "The Little Calf" is reminiscent of Mendele Mocher Sforim and Sholem Aleichem in its concern for
the natural life of the senses that is so briefly enjoyed by Jewish children. The child's attachment to the domestic animal
is thwarted by the priorities of the Jewish reality that cannot
afford such happy and generous impulses. In several works
Blinken develops the prominent *Haskalah* theme of shackled
individuality and creative pleasure.

The novella "Women," one of the author's most effective
works, is a poetic evocation of the market women of his native town. A collective portrait of East European *shtetl* life, it
bears a close resemblance to Sholem Asch's study, *The Shtetl*,
in which sections of Jewish small-town society are presented
in their corporate form, as if the author were trying to fix a
group portrait that could never be reassembled thereafter. Into
this collective portrait Blinken introduces a moment of individual abuse and shame, for which the market women, in in-
spiring solidarity, seek atonement.

On the other side of the ledger, some of Blinken's own influence on his fellow writers can be seen through his story
"Smoke," which traces the dissolution of a marriage based on
false impressions. The young man who spoke idealistically
about raising children, when he hears that his wife is preg-

nant, counsels an abortion because they are not yet ready. His smoking becomes for her the palpable symbol of his inconstancy and shallowness—"smoke, it's all just so much smoke." The young wife resolves to leave her husband and raise the child herself. Five years later, the Yiddish writer Lamed Shapiro wrote one of his loveliest stories under the same title and with the same motif. In his story, too, the life of husband and wife is interpreted through the act of smoking, but Shapiro inverts its meaning to represent virility and temporal enjoyment. Whether consciously or not, Shapiro reworked elements of Blinken's story for his own artistic ends.

During these years of eager experimentation, Blinken tried his hand at various subjects and genres of short fiction, some of them represented in this volume. He was fascinated by the volatile interaction between men and women, and this attraction he explored both for its own sake and for the insight it yielded about the elemental nature of the human being. Given the inwardness of the *yunge*, and the programmatic interest of most of the writers and poets in states of feeling, this subject was by no means Blinken's alone, but there was no Yiddish writer of the period with such subtle or concentrated attention. This is perhaps the area of his major achievement and influence.

Meir Blinken's death in 1915, just before his thirty-sixth birthday, cut short, in the words of one obituary, "the development of an artistic talent and the high hopes that were held for him in Jewish literary circles of America." One indication of the high esteem in which he was held was the public funeral accorded him on the steps of the *Jewish Daily Forward* on East Broadway, where he was eulogized by prominent colleagues.

Since most of his contemporaries required a long period of literary apprenticeship before they produced their finest work, we must assume that Blinken, too, still had his finest work before him. His great self-confidence as a writer, his demonstrated stamina, and his progressive gravitation toward longer forms of fiction suggest that he would surely have gone on to write novels, as his fellow writers Joseph Opatoshu and Isaac Raboy began to do at just about this time. A decade of acclimatization was evidently required before these immigrant Yiddish artists had gained sufficient comfort and facility in their new surroundings to produce their best work. By the time of his death Blinken was already one of the boldest and most mature of the prose writers, and we readers no less than Blinken's contemporaries may have reason to mourn his untimely death, just as he had hit his stride.

For several years, Blinken continued to be cited as one of the major voices among the *yunge*, but he was gradually forgotten and his work neglected. It was Blinken's son, fifteen years old at the time of his father's death, who determined to put out a collection of his father's fiction and to make at least part of it available as well in English translation. This he has done, not merely as an act of filial piety, but out of his own strong commitment to American pluralism, and to its Jewish cultural component. A lifelong activist in the cause of Zionism, first in its promotion and lately in its defense, M. H. Blinken has long been concerned with the importance of history, of our true understanding of the past, in attempting an intelligent approach to the present. This book intends to broaden our awareness of the culture of our past by introducing a Yiddish writer of the pre−World War I period who was already torn by many of the tensions and conflicts that continue to be ours.

Stories by Meir Blinkin

Card Game

I   THE PRETTY young woman, in the full bloom of life and vigor, strode impatiently around the room. Stopping more and more frequently at the window, she opened it wide and stuck her head out. An angry wind insolently slapped her face, trying to shove her back. When she refused to submit, the wind tousled and tangled her long blonde hair. This bothered her very little, however; Fanya was not one to let the wind get the better of her. She merely wrapped her hair in a kerchief and leaned even further out the window.

As far as her eye could see, spread out before her lay a white, sparkling—in some places untrodden—blanket of fresh snow. Was that someone walking out there? Yes, it was Moyshe! No, it wasn't! Why was he so late today? Usually her husband came home punctually, but always she grew impatient as she waited. All day long she was alone, and when he finally did come home he still couldn't find any time to spend with her.

To punish him for being so late, she would play a trick on him, but first she would get dressed. She put on her new almond-colored dress with the pink collar, combed her hair in an upsweep and tied it in a sky-blue ribbon. Admiring herself in the mirror, it occurred to her to slip on her favorite little beige apron, which made her look even more charming, younger, almost childlike.

What could she do to trick him?

It had to be something that would make him laugh. When he rang the doorbell, she wouldn't answer. Let him think she wasn't home. No, that was no good! She would leave the door open just a crack and hide somewhere. But suppose he were bringing someone home with him for dinner? No, that was no good, either. . . . Aha! She would put on her morning-robe, wrap a towel around her head and act sleepy. Finding her in her robe that way, Moyshe would naturally believe she had been asleep and that his ringing had awakened her. He would wink at her and motion to her to go back into the bedroom and get dressed. She would act the innocent—what was he trying to tell her? "Fanyetchke," he would say, "what's wrong with you?" Then she would make a sudden movement as if to take off her robe. "What are you doing!" he would exclaim in alarm, seizing her hand. "Fanyetchka, why are you acting so strangely today?"

Only then would she throw off her robe, pull the towel from her head, and there she'd be—all dressed up! Oh, would he look silly, standing there with his mouth wide open!

Meanwhile, as she was imagining the scene, she heard her husband's footsteps on the stairs. She ran to the door and listened. Recognizing his tread, she hastily got into her robe, deftly wound a towel around her head and skipped back to the door. She opened it a little and waited eagerly, enjoying her prank. Even before Moyshe touched the electric button, she opened the door wide and with a saucy, radiant smile, greeted him:

"So you finally came home, you bad boy!"

Moyshe was about to scold her for coming to the door half-undressed—one of these days she would catch a bad cold that way—but before he could utter a word, Fanya loosened her robe with a flourish and, wrapping it around him, marched playfully into the dining room, pulling him along.

As she helped her husband remove his overcoat, Fanya brazenly put her hands into his pockets where he usually kept the gifts he bought for her.

"Look at her! And I was worried you were naked!"

"Why? What did you have in mind?" she grinned.

In response, Moyshe touched Fanya's flaming cheeks with his fingertips. She sprang back with a mock little scream.

"Oh, you wicked man! Have mercy!"

"Cold?"

She put a reproachful look on her face.

Gazing at his wife appreciatively, Moyshe smiled. His eyes had that particularly contented look of a happy man who thinks highly of himself but is nonetheless ready to admit that there are no human beings on earth without shortcomings and that he might even have a few himself.

"And what if your husband doesn't bring home a present once in a while—does that mean the world's coming to an end? Is that any reason to sulk?" He made a brave effort to sound stern, but Fanya burst into a loud and cheerful laugh.

"You're not angry with me, Fanyetchka?"

"Don't be a silly man!"

"Why do you call me silly?"

"Just so—no reason. . . ."

"No reason? What kind of answer is that?"

"Just tell me one thing, Mister Manilov, why are you so late today?"

"Sounds like you miss me a lot, yes?"

"Not you so much, Mister, as your presents!"

"Oh, so that's it? Well, well, now you're the one who's acting silly! Can't you take a joke anymore?"

"My whole life is a big joke!"

Moyshe looked at her gravely. "Tell me, Missus Manilov, in what college did you study philosophy?"

No longer able to resist his smile, she replied fondly: "When the husband is a philosopher, some of it rubs off on the wife!"

Moyshe moved closer, as if to inspect her apron, but in the same gesture, slipped his arm around her waist.

"What a delicious morsel you are, Fanya!"

"Behave yourself, Manilov!"

"You can't imagine how cold it is out there today, Fan-yetchka!"

"Downtown it's just as cold as out here?"

"The cold I can live with, but the *tumel*, the rushing around, God Almighty! I tell you, Fanya, people just step all over each other! And not only on the sidewalks—even in the middle of the street you can get your ribs crushed!"

He must be telling her this now for a reason, Fanya sensed.

"Why is it worse now than usual?"

"It's not worse. I'll just never get used to it!" He picked up an end of the bread from the table and started chewing.

"Hungry, Moyshe?"

"You need to ask? I'm hungry as ten lions!"

Fanya ran into the kitchen. He used the opportunity to take a pair of expensive, fur-lined gloves out of his breast pocket. Tiptoeing into the bedroom, he laid the gloves on the dresser and quietly returned to the dining room just before Fanya reappeared, carrying a white porcelain dish which emitted puffs of hot steam.

"I cooked your favorite meal today, Moyshe."

"How did you know?"

"How did I know what?"

"What I wanted."

"Silly, who should know better?"

"You cooked a hot borscht?"

"And stuffed chicken necks, too!" Fanya winked.

"You're worth your weight in gold, Fanya!"

"And you're worth your weight in silver," she joked.

"Moyshele—" she began, with a note of pleading in her tone.

"What is it now, Missus Philosopher?"

"Will you play cards with me this evening?"

"I'm too busy tonight, darling."

"Busy, busy, always busy!"

"If I have to work, I have to!"

"You always have to! When *don't* you have to? But you have to live, too, don't you?"

"You think life consists only of poker and pinochle?"

Offended, she said nothing. She had a right to feel hurt. To begin with, it wasn't fair of him to accuse her of playing poker or pinochle when she didn't even know how to play those games. Secondly, he was the one who had introduced her to cards and taught her casino. Before that she hadn't known the difference between a club and a spade! Thirdly and most important, she really didn't have any friends to help her pass the time. And whose fault was that, if not his?

To Moyshe, however, it seemed that she was grumbling mainly because he hadn't kept his promise to bring home his friend Yudin, who was not only a man of culture but an expert card player. Moyshe could not restrain a smile as Fanya complained, "I'm not really living."

His smile did not amuse her. She flinched, almost as if he'd raised a hand to strike her. Worried, he tried to smooth the whole thing over by announcing confidently:

"All right, Fanyetchka! Tomorrow I'm bringing home Mister Yudin and you'll have a friend to pass the time with!"

"You don't have to do it for my sake—it makes no difference to me one way or the other!"

Now her tone alarmed him even more. He hoped she wouldn't burst into tears and begin her litany of complaints: he had locked her in a gilded cage, all day long she never saw another human being, she was not a cow who needs nothing more out of life than its feed, etc., etc. He'd been hearing those words more and more often from Fanya recently, and since he knew that a great deal of what she said was close to the truth, he preferred not to hear them again.

"Sweetheart, please bring me my pen and ink—I've got to write a few letters. When I'm finished we'll play cards for a while. Can I help it if I've got to do everything myself? You know the old saying: the only good thing you can do with other people's hands is to gather hot coals."

Fanya went to fetch his writing implements but took so long to return that he grew impatient. Suddenly she let out such a loud squeal that it startled him. He rushed toward the bedroom. Not until she called his name delightedly did he remember about the gloves.

"Oh, you big bluffer! Trying to hide your present—"

"You like those gloves, Fanyetchke?"

She looked at him affectionately and then, as though something were impelling her, ran to him and breathlessly covered his face with kisses.

"You know I'm right, don't you! Is it a disgrace to play cards in your own home? Show me one house on this street where they don't play casino, pinochle, whist—or even poker! Haven't you been telling me yourself to invite Mrs. Resnick and her friends over to teach me the game of whist? Didn't you tell me that? Meantime, until they teach me, you've got to play with me. If you don't have time now, we won't play. But why scold me? What have I done to deserve that?"

She spoke with so much honest feeling that he was deeply moved. He looked at her tenderly for a long moment, his eyes free of any carnal passion, and reminded himself that he really wasn't the angel she imagined him to be, that she was a much finer person than he would ever be. For the first time he felt emotions of profound respect and esteem for her. He was happy and proud, not because she was his wife and belonged to him alone, but because she was his friend, in all her blameless innocence, and trusted him so implicitly.

And while these thoughts elevated her even higher in his esteem, they only made him feel worse about himself. Her integrity was a cutting indictment of his much-too-clever dishonesty, a condemnation of all his negative thoughts about his wife. Could a woman's virtue become a burden to her husband? If he could find a way to tell her something of what he was thinking, perhaps he wouldn't feel so ashamed of himself.

As they went to bed that night, Fanya said half in jest: "If we ever have a daughter, I'll never let her marry a businessman, Moyshele!"

"Why not, Fanyetchka?"

"Because—"

"Am I such a bad husband?"

Uncertain how to answer him, she buried her head in his shoulder and fell asleep.

That night she dreamed that Moyshe had brought home his *landsman*, a creature with long, skinny arms that reached almost to the ground. She awoke in terror, spit three times to ward off the evil spirits, and soon fell fast asleep again.

A sunbeam, creeping into the room around a folded edge of the curtain, awakened her.

Sensing the sun's warmth on her body, Fanya sat up happily, her heart as light and carefree as a child's on the first day of spring. As though she were recalling a pleasurable incident, a tranquil smile illuminated her face.

Fully awake now and feeling energetic, she began her housecleaning. For several hours she worked at a lively pace—sweeping, scrubbing, polishing—until every corner sparkled. Intent on finishing her chores, she kept putting off lunch until a sharp hunger-pang forced her to stop and swallow a few bites of food. Then she started dressing. For a long time she stood staring absently into the mirror, moved by some mysterious urge to dress up in all her finery today. Several times she combed her hair, uncombed it and recombed it again. In the midst of all this, a neighbor who came in to borrow something asked her why she was getting "all dolled up" in the middle of the day. Again not knowing why, Fanya felt her gorge rise as she responded angrily:

"Must I have a special reason? Must we always look sloppy just because we're housewives? It wouldn't hurt you to spend a little more time on your own appearance once in a while!" The neighbor left in a huff.

Regretting her unwonted outburst, she finished her toilet and began fixing supper. She knew she should serve something special in honor of their guest, but instead she found herself preparing a very simple meal, with her mind only half on her work. Her thoughts had gone to their guest and from him to Mrs. Resnick. Whenever Moyshe mentioned Sadie Resnick his tone indicated that she was somehow not a very respectable woman and that he disliked her intensely. Yet on those few occasions when Mrs. Resnick had visited them he had greeted her in a manner so friendly that he seemed genuinely glad to see her. The last time that had happened, Moyshe said to Fanya after their guests left:

"Fanyetchke, I want you to know that to me you're a very special person. I wouldn't exchange a thousand Sadie Resnicks for one of your footsteps. Women like her should consider themselves honored that you even speak to them."

But his "compliment" did not sit too well with Fanya. Why did he always refer to Mrs. Resnick in such a hostile way? If she were really the kind of woman he described, why was he so eager for his own wife to become friendly with her? What did she need friends like that for? He himself ought not to permit it. . . .

2   Moyshe and Fanya have now been married three years. She is a strikingly beautiful woman, slender and graceful. Over her clear, sunny face flits a saucy innocence. All her features are comely and charming. Her blue eyes are dreamy, her long throat smooth and white, her blonde hair soft, curly and abundant. Everything about her, every movement, every gesture, is a gentle, tender chord of wholesome youth. It was her beauty that had attracted Moyshe, yet three years ago, when they were married, Fanya had not been as pretty as she is now. Her body—too thin for his taste—made him think of a rose before it unfolds.

On the other hand, Moyshe, eight years older than his wife, had been better looking *before* they were married. About the same height as Fanya, he was sturdily built, his face ruddy, his eyes intelligent, alert and always searching.

A well-to-do young man, he soon came to believe that there wasn't even one woman in the world good enough for him, and he therefore began paying special attention to Fanya, a lonely girl with no family in America. Moyshe reasoned this way: She was still very young. The "shop" had not yet placed its debilitating stamp upon her. She was so isolated and alone in the new country that if he, a prosperous businessman, were to marry her, she would be grateful to him forever. The only blemish he saw in her was that she was a bit too lean, but he hoped that, secure in his home, living in luxury, she would soon put on some weight, look more robust. Never one to procrastinate, he made Fanya a proposal of marriage.

Fanya refused to believe her ears. Moyshe wanted her? How could she compare to him? A handsome, successful young fellow, in the prime of life, he could demand a dowry of at least five thousand dollars. She hadn't a penny to her name. He couldn't be serious.

When he finally convinced her that he really meant it, she accepted happily. And very soon after the wedding, Fanya began looking healthier, even more beautiful. Wherever Moyshe appeared with her, men stared so shamelessly that it began to prey on his mind. He even grew so exasperated with his own cousins and uncles for being too chummy with Fanya that he stopped visiting them. More than anything else he worried lest she find out how desirable a woman she actually was. It would not be good for her to know that men could not help devouring her with their eyes.

The better Moyshe's business affairs went and the more love Fanya gave him, the more uneasy he became, without understanding why. It became almost a ritual with him to ask her how much she loved him, whether she would always be true to him, and so forth. These interrogations usually took place after they went to bed.

"Do you love me as much now as when we were first married?"

"No Moyshe! A thousand times more!"

"Will you love me that way always, Fanyetchke?"

"Always, Moyshele, always and forever!"

"And suppose I took sick and died?"

"Don't talk that way, it scares me!"

"Will you always be faithful to me?"

"I will be only yours, Moyshe, always. Always the first and the last, I will be yours. . . ."

Moyshe understood her to mean: *you* will be *mine* first and last, but he never corrected her. On the contrary, the more often he heard it from her, the more precious the sound of the words became, because they came out of her heart, even if she didn't realize their significance. He was certain that she spoke the truth.

These conversations with Fanya made him very happy, but it was only a momentary happiness. The following morning he was already imagining that his wife was thinking about someone else, that she had a secret lover, that she was deliberately answering his questions in a way calculated to mislead him, to allay his fears. And again the worm of doubt would start gnawing at him. His fits of jealousy left him more weary than if he'd been doing hard physical labor.

When it became impossible for Moyshe to go on living with this unremitting fear and uncertainty, he began looking for some way to relieve these anxieties that overwhelmed him during the long days he was away from home. And it seemed to him that he needed this not so much for his sake as for the sake of another being that dwelled inside him, someone whom he had to convince of Fanya's purity, of her trustworthiness. Perhaps he ought to move out to a suburb, far out in the Bronx, rent an entire floor for himself and Fanya, decorate it with the best and most modern furnishings. Complete responsibility for the care of her home would keep Fanya so busy she wouldn't have time for anyone or anything else. Moreover, life in the Bronx, not as exciting as in New York City, would have fewer temptations.

And since Moyshe rarely put off doing anything that entered his head, they were soon located in a new home. Whatever Fanya liked, he bought, without asking any questions.

His calculations proved correct. At first, Fanya had so much to do—what with the cleaning and the cooking—that she could barely finish her work during the course of the day. Moyshe was quite content with the arrangement. His jealousy, which had been tormenting him like an unrelieved toothache, diminished significantly. Feeling more at ease, he again turned his full attention to ways of making his business more profitable.

Every evening, sometimes at a late hour, Fanya waited eagerly for her husband's return. But even before he finished his meal—if he didn't fall asleep at the table—he sat down to write business letters or check his accounts, leaving Fanya to sit alone, bored and aggrieved, her eyes brimming, as she waited patiently, without knowing exactly what she was waiting for. More than once Moyshe said to her, not even raising his eyes from the paper in front of him:

"Fanyetchke, why don't you go to bed? It's getting late."

She would burst out crying and flee into the bedroom, lonely and dejected. Then Moyshe would apologize and kiss her and Fanya would immediately forgive him and feel better.

And that's how it went for months and months until finally his behavior forced her to speak out. One evening, gathering up all her courage, she said:

"You know, Moyshe, I truly envy those women who are poor and who can't live in a fine house like mine."

"And why is that, Fanya?"

"Because at least they can enjoy themselves with their husbands once in a while. . . ."

Her simple words frightened him. Attaching a much deeper significance to them than she had actually intended, he started taking Fanya with him to his store every morning. But here his troubles began afresh. Almost from the very first day that Fanya appeared in the store, his employees lost all sense of propriety. No sooner did Fanya arrive in the morning than they swarmed around her like bees around honey. Their conversation—including their jokes—was only about her. Moyshe would boil and simmer, but had to act as if he didn't see what was going on right under his nose.

It was even worse when the store filled up with customers and the clerks were touting the merchandise. At such times one could hear remarks like these:

"Mister, our goods is the best, I should only live so long! Did you ever see such merchandise anywhere? So marvelously put together it's perfect! Look at it!" As the salespeople ogled the boss's wife they swore on their grandmother's grave that this "piece of goods" was "A-number-one."

These shenanigans put the clerks in a wonderful mood. They could say out loud whatever they felt about Fanya. And quite often the customer would join in and agree that the quality of the "merchandise" under discussion was obviously unquestionable. The conversation would grow even more picturesque, with the clerk and the customer laughing uproariously over their secret joke. And all the while, Moyshe, acting as if he didn't understand a thing, burned hotter and hotter inside, at the clerks, at the customers, at himself, at the world.

"Why doesn't she stay out of their sight, why can't she understand, that little fool, that they are talking about her?"

But all Fanya had to do was look at him with her innocent, uncorrupted eyes and Moyshe forgave her everything. He was even glad she didn't understand their vulgar innuendos; it only proved how unsullied she was. Nevertheless, he had no choice but to stop bringing her to the store. If she started complaining again, then they would decide what to do. In the meantime, if she didn't show up in the store every day, it would put a stop to his constant battling with his employees. If it weren't so hard to replace them, he'd have fired a couple of them long ago, the damn fools!

And in order that Fanya should stop complaining, Moyshe taught her the game of casino, the only card game he knew. Purposely coming home earlier, he played cards with her every evening after supper. Whenever she won a game he promised her a present, and usually kept his word.

Fanya was delighted with her husband's new attitude. Almost every evening she had his attention, at least for a while. It cheered her up immeasurably.

3 Moyshe came home without Yudin. Fanya felt a sharp pang of disappointment. What could it mean? Was her husband still jealous?

She decided to confront him directly. But the right moment did not arise. It might be better to wait until Moyshe broached the subject himself.

A couple of weeks passed, however, and he avoided talking about it. Outwardly it appeared that the whole matter was closed, that both husband and wife had put it out of their minds. The truth was, of course, that neither of them had forgotten, least of all Fanya. She had even invented conversations and incidents between Yudin and herself. She pictured him as a tall, strong, good-looking young man with dark curly hair, burning black eyes, and a voice like a lion.

These imaginary conversations went something like this.

Midafternoon. She is cleaning house, is not properly attired. A knock at the door.

"Who's there?" she calls.

"It's Yudin!" an unfamiliar voice replies.

She lets him in, runs to the bedroom. "Have a seat, Mr. Yudin, I'll be there in a moment! Please excuse me!"

"Certainly, certainly!" His booming voice fills the whole house with love.

Dressing quickly, she comes out to greet him. Yudin stands up, smiles gently, almost intimately.

"How are you, Mrs. Manilov?"

"So you're *the* Mr. Yudin, my husband's *landsman*?"

"Yes, ma'm, that's me!"

"If I'm not mistaken, you were supposed to have been here a couple of weeks ago?"

"Yes, I was. Manilov had arranged to pick me up on his way home—he has to pass my place—but he didn't stop."

"May I ask how you happen to be here today?"

Her visitor blushes.

"I've been wanting very much to meet you, Mrs. Manilov. But if Moyshe didn't stop for me that day, he must have forgotten. He's such a busy man. So I decided to come here on my own. . . ."

Another fantasy of Fanya's:

She and Moyshe are downtown, on the way to the theater. Arriving at the theater, they are greeted by a tall, strapping young man with dark, flaming eyes. He shakes hands first with her, then with her husband.

"Can you perhaps explain to me, Mrs. Manilov, why your esteemed husband refuses to show you off to the rest of the world?" As he says this, he looks at Moyshe and smiles.

"Really, Mrs. Manilov, so many times I've begged him to introduce me to you! He keeps promising to do so, but never keeps his word."

"My Moyshe always keeps his word. But his business takes up all his time. He has to do everything himself. You know what they say: 'With other people's hands it's easy to gather hot coals. . . .'"

After a while Moyshe realized that he had acted childishly in not bringing Yudin home with him. No one had forced him to suggest that he bring home his friend, but once he had done so, he should have kept his promise. He must find a way to straighten this whole thing out, once and for all. One evening, while playing casino with Fanya, he commented warily:

"You know, it's a funny thing. I used to see him almost every day, but now—just in spite—he doesn't show up anywhere. . . ."

Fanya put down a card and waited, as if she hadn't even heard him.

"I wonder if he's angry with me or something? Tomorrow for sure I'm going to drop in on him."

"I don't know who you're talking about, Moyshe," Fanya murmured as she studied her cards.

Her too casual disclaimer struck Moyshe like an unexpected blow. It could only mean that she, too, had been thinking about Yudin. He didn't know how to reply to her, how to extract himself from an embarrassing situation.

He tossed out a nine of spades.

"There's a five and a four on the table, Moyshe. . . ."

His fingers trembled as he gathered in the three cards.

"Maybe you're too tired tonight, Moyshe. Let's put the cards away and go to bed."

Moyshe slept fitfully and woke up much earlier than usual. He tried so hard not to awaken Fanya that it made her suspicious. Not until he had drunk half a tumbler of cognac and chased it down with a piece of cake—his morning habit—did Fanya feel calmer.

All day long she had a sense that something unusual was going to happen, that the matter would not pass over so smoothly. With mounting anxiety she awaited her husband's homecoming. Her heart had not misled her. Moyshe arrived with Yudin in tow. Seeing them together, Fanya lost her customary equanimity and did not know what to do first. She found herself in the comical situation of a person who has so much to do and so little time to do it in that she does nothing. Of all days, she was unprepared, had not even dusted the furniture. Why hadn't he warned her he was bringing home a guest? She was surprised, frightened, yet strangely elated at the same time.

"Fanyetchke! Where the devil are you hiding? Come out and meet a good friend of mine!"

Slipping into a fresh blouse, she came back into the dining room.

"Fanya, this is my old friend Yudin!"

"I'm very happy to meet you," Yudin said, looking as if he meant it. In truth, he was a bit nervous himself. In his life he had never met such a beautiful Jewish woman. He could not take his eyes off her face.

In turn, his look made Fanya blush, as though his eyes were kissing her, caressing her, drawing her to him like a magnet. She pulled back her shoulders and gave him an embarrassed smile. How could he be doing this to her when he was so far away? Why did she feel as if his arms were tightening around her?

She took a deep breath. "Moyshe, why don't you and your friend sit in the parlor for a bit while I get things ready here?"

A few minutes later she invited them back into the dining room. The table was laden with a variety of tasty dishes. The men sipped their cognac slowly and talked. Not until they had each finished a third glass did Moyshe notice that Fanya was not at the table.

"Fanya," he called out guiltily, "why don't you come and eat with us?"

"I'm not hungry tonight, Moyshe!"

"I'm sure I wasn't expected—" Yudin apologized lamely.

"There's always something in our house to eat, thank God," Fanya managed to say.

Eventually Yudin involved her in the conversation. Why did he no longer see her in Moyshe's store, he wanted to know, or for that matter, anywhere else. Not knowing how to answer, Fanya looked to her husband for help.

"With such a household on her shoulders, it's no joke . . . she's usually too busy to go out. . . ." Moyshe tried to explain.

His "explanation" made Fanya laugh to herself, though she saw nothing funny in it.

Yudin didn't stay long. His good-bye was equally cordial to both his host and hostess.

"Why so early?" Moyshe objected. "We haven't even cut the cards yet!"

"Next time," Yudin suggested, glancing at Fanya.

"To tell you the truth," she said, "Moyshe has told me so much about you that I'd be afraid to play with you. . . ."

"Is that so? What kind of nonsense has he been telling you?"

All she could do was beam at her husband.

"That's very nice, my friend, making your wife afraid of me before she even meets me!" Yudin complained.

"Well, I didn't tell her any lies. Anyway, one has to be careful nowadays, even with a friend!"

"You don't say! Good night to you both!"

"Good night! Come and see us again soon, Mr. Yudin."

"She's right, Yudin," seconded Moyshe. "Don't wait for a special invitation!"

But the idea wouldn't let Moyshe rest. Suppose his friend did come to visit during the day. They would be all alone, just the two of them. Unnerving thoughts invaded his head. Not that he had anything against Yudin. What terrible stories had he heard that he should be suspicious of him? All he knew was that Yudin was a "college man" who somehow never let him forget that fact. Actually they spent very little time together, and whenever they did meet, Yudin managed to keep the conversation on matters that even a child would have found easy to understand. Maybe he meant no harm by it, but Moyshe did not think it very complimentary. Outside of that, he had no complaints whatsoever against Yudin. If only he weren't one of those radicals who believes that what's yours is mine and what's God's is everybody's!

Moyshe smiled inwardly. Sadie Resnick had once warned him to "keep an eye" on his wife, because she was "such a rare dish." What a vulgar woman she was, that Resnick, but still, a clever wench. "Wives like yours," she had advised him, "are about as safe with any normal young man as a keg of gunpowder in a burning cellar!"

And Yudin was certainly a "normal" young man. But what a foolish thought! Fanya wouldn't exchange her husband for any other man on earth! Fanya was the epitome of fidelity. It's true what people say: the thief always feels that everybody's eyes are on *him*. Fanya was a respectable woman and Yudin was an honorable man. Nevertheless it would be plainly improper for him to visit with Fanya when her husband wasn't at home. Why give gossips such a juicy item to chew on?

The following day Moyshe paid Sadie Resnick a visit. He would offer his home for her card games if they would teach his wife to play. On several occasions Sadie had hinted that it would be more fitting if Fanya herself invited them. He was not too keen on the whole idea, but after all, what damage could they do? They wouldn't bite chunks out of the furniture.

She came to the door in a half-unbuttoned housecoat.

"Manilov! What are you doing here in the middle of the day? I'm just getting dressed to go out."

"I felt like visiting an old friend."

"Still the same old bluffer!"

She went back into her bedroom, followed closely by Moyshe. He patted her behind.

"Glutton! The one you have at home isn't enough for you?"

Moyshe grinned as she took off the housecoat. He leaped toward her round, full breasts.

"Careful, Manilov!"

"My hands are nice and warm, Resnick!"

"Save your warm hands for somebody else! Does your Fanya have a lover yet?"

"She doesn't believe in such things."

"She doesn't believe? Since when is it a religion? Does the little fool also believe that only husbands have the right?"

He put his hands behind him in mock submissiveness as she pressed his head to her bosom.

"Tell me the truth for a change, Manilov! What *are* you doing here?"

"Can't you see what I'm doing?"

"Your wife is younger and prettier than me—"

"It's for her sake that I'm here."

"Liar!"

"It's the truth!"

"Then why didn't you bring her along?"

"She's been after me for months to invite you and your friends to our home. Why don't we see you anymore? Our home is always open to you, Sadie."

Her eyes lit up. "If she really wants us to come, all right. She won't have much time to play cards when she starts having kids. What's taking you so long, anyway?"

"Don't worry, they'll come."

"But Fanya still has no one else?"

"Don't spoil it for me!"

"Scared, ha? I still don't understand why you're allowed and she isn't. Don't look so nervous, Manilov, I'm only teasing. I won't ruin your merchandise!"

"Then it's agreed? You'll come?"

"Certainly! With pleasure!"

She stretched out to her full height, opening up her firm, white arms.

He covered her throat with kisses, pushing her toward a couch.

"Not now, Manilov! I told you—I'm on my way—"

"Be a sport, Sadie!"

"Not on your life! Don't do that! Not now—"

Her objections grew weaker and weaker.

"Well, Sadie, when shall we expect you?"

"Today's Monday—let me see—we'll be there on Thursday—"

The two "good friends" said good-bye affectionately, but as Moyshe left, he was not at all pleased with himself. He had grown unaccustomed to such "trysts" and now his conduct seemed ugly and demeaning even to him.

At home he told Fanya that Mrs. Resnick had come into the store to shop and that in the presence of others she had embarrassed him by calling him a miser who's afraid to have people come to his home. So he'd had no choice but to invite her and her friends for a nice sociable game. Fanya kissed him, thanked him happily and did not even ask him to play cards with her that evening.

"Actually, Fanyetchka, I've been hoping this would happen, for your sake. It just seemed beneath my dignity somehow to invite her. But since it happened this way—"

Moyshe made Fanya promise that she would never go to Mrs. Resnick's to play, because it was not befitting her station in life. Having thus protected himself, he was now rather more pleased than less with the way things were going. And Fanya, delighted that she would soon have a new circle of friends, was especially happy that her husband was showing some concern about her enforced boredom and was finally doing something to relieve it.

4 The big day arrived. Five women, with Mrs. Sadie Resnick at their head, came to visit Fanya Manilov. They made friends with her very quickly, that is, they recognized immediately that they had "caught a real bargain." And this was something they urgently needed. For her part, Fanya was very grateful. After all, she hadn't known any of them well, except that she had met Mrs. Resnick a few times and heard many amusing stories about Mrs. Kaplan.

The four women that Mrs. Resnick introduced to her were: Sophie Kaplan, Claire LaFontaine, Betty Smith and Jennie Cyril. And although the last three of those names do not have a particularly Jewish ring, it should be noted for the sake of truth that they were all authentically Jewish women.

Two others were absent from the usual "set." Why they were not there we shall reveal later.

The oldest of the group is Sadie Resnick, who had become their leader because of her many "contacts." Forty-three or forty-four years old, tall, well-endowed and vigorous, Sadie bleaches her hair and looks five years younger. She has been in America about twenty-four years, and almost from her first day here has never lacked for friends. She had a definite talent for making friends in the old days. People found it easy to lend her a helping hand, especially since she had come to this country all alone.

For these favors she repaid her friends generously. From two of them she took their husbands. In those cases where she was unsuccessful in accomplishing this, she at least managed to create bad feelings between husband and wife. When it came to gossip, she was an expert. More than one woman had shed bitter tears because of her. But Sadie Resnick couldn't care less.

And if the truth be told, she did not do these things out of malice. It was that kind of time in this country—traces of it are still present today—a time which gave rise to a certain class of people whose life's work consisted in doing whatever their hearts desired, whenever they desired it. Should any member of this class have said, for example, that it was wrong to sleep with the husband of your best friend, or with the wife of your best friend, such a person would have been branded a coward or a small-town yokel who did not know how to get the most out of life. The more affairs and experiences you had, the better was your reputation, the greater the esteem in which you were held.

Sadie Resnick (she had chosen to keep her maiden name) is the most typical representative of that class. For a long time—actually it wasn't too long ago—she had been intimate with Moyshe, and she was then already married to her present husband. But as we say, she did this not out of malice but just for the fun of doing it. Moyshe was young, strong, handsome and not stingy with the dollar. So what? Was she hurting anyone? Even now the gossip is that she is "having a good time" with her husband's younger brother, but why believe the fabrications of malicious tongues?

Sadie very rarely speaks about her past—with strangers, that is. With people she can trust, she is quite candid. She denies nothing and will tell you proudly how this or that leader of the Jewish labor movement once kneeled like a supplicant at her feet and if she had ordered him to climb up on the table and crow like a rooster, he'd have done so without hesitation. Even today, whenever such a man runs into her somewhere, he trembles like a schoolboy.

Today she laughs at all of them and will tell you: "You've got to know how to live in this world!" With these words, in fact, she usually climaxes her conversations about "the good old days."

Second in command is Claire LaFontaine, a strong, attractive woman of medium height, blonde, with lively brown eyes and an impish smile. It is very difficult to judge her age, especially because—as she herself will tell you—on every birthday she feels a year younger.

Almost as soon as she got her job in a dress factory, they made her a forelady. Having become a big-shot in such short order, she did not treat the working women in her section very honorably. Luckily, the wives of the bosses and the foremen soon sensed, almost magically, that a destructive, satanic spirit had infiltrated the place and would poison their lives if they didn't do something about it in a hurry. So they did. They had her fired.

Claire LaFontaine lived openly with every boss who ever employed her, and she did it defiantly, thereby demonstrating her independent free spirit. If a manufacturer ever dismissed her from her job, it didn't faze her in the least. She was never out of work. She was always in demand. The workers said cynically that "LaFontaine owns all of Broadway," since she had slept with every factory owner on that street at one time or another. With a wink they would add that she also had a few clients in Philadelphia "on the side."

None of this, however, prevented her from marrying a wealthy banker and living with him in style. The difference between her and Sadie Resnick is that Sadie had married as a divorcée and Claire as a "maiden."

There are many stories current about the origin of her name. A certain playboy lawyer explained that however one pronounces LaFontaine, one should always add "de Canada," because although she had never been in France, she had spent four months in Montreal as a nurse and must have had something to do with a French-Canadian.

The way she herself tells it, though, her father's brother, who had been conscripted into the Russian army, had by some fluke landed in France and eventually become Count de la Fontaine. After his death they found a will which provided that at the end of fifty years his entire estate should go to whatever members of the family still bore his name. So there were a number of Jewish LaFontaines scattered around the world.

In a sense, Sophie Kaplan is more interesting than any of them. Tall and slender, she appears to be around forty-five, though she is actually four years younger. Her face is so pallid and her eyes so lifeless that she resembles a faded photograph. The words that come out of her mouth, however, are usually sharp and amusing. Sophie is one of those patriotic Jews who swears that she has never in her life had any dealings with non-Jewish men, and that she never will.

Her husband, who made his money in real estate, is much older than she is, so she persuaded him to sign half of all his possessions over to her name. After the legal papers were all signed and sealed, Sophie stole his son away from his young wife, drove out the old man, and is now prominent in the wealthy circles of the city.

Sophie Kaplan is not a "big talker," so no one knows the whole truth about her past life. And since she isn't very pretty, people assume she must have had an unhappy childhood. Perhaps that's why she got into the habit of keeping silent. Now she is very active in charitable causes, contributes large sums of money, is vice president of two societies, and receives high praise in the English and Yiddish press for philanthropic services to the community.

She has, however, one failing: when she plays cards—it doesn't matter whether with women or with men—she is prone to coarse, filthy language. At such times, looking at her stony face, on which not a muscle moves, it is impossible to believe that such words are coming out of her mouth.

Betty Smith, though an ordinary flirt, is no doubt a very beautiful one. Forty-three years old, she looks twenty-five. Slightly taller than average, blonde, with a longe white neck and blue, sparkling eyes, her skin is so clear and delicate that men go wild just looking at her.

Lively and loquacious, she speaks with everyone about anything and everything, becomes a "good buddy" in a moment. She has the knack of making an admirer out of any man she chooses, even the kind of man who doesn't know the first thing about what women are for. She whispers such intimacies to these admirers that their heads are soon whirling. And she utters these intimacies not so much with her lips as with the soft fingers of her hands, with her shapely hips, with the tips of her dainty shoes, with her curly blonde hair, with her tempting breasts that breathe fire.

Her admirers, lovers or sympathizers—whatever one chooses to call them—always believe, at their very first meeting with her, that everything is "in the bag," because she permits them to tell her whatever is in their hearts.

She keeps her appointments punctually and doesn't object if her "boyfriends" try to kiss her. But as soon as any one of them begins to demonstrate the "irresistible force of his desires," he soon finds out he is not in control at all. She only laughs at their helplessness, enjoying their frustrations. Even with her own husband she is like a cat toying with a mouse. The name "Smith," by the way, is not her fault. It came with her husband.

Jennie Cyril, the fifth member of our group, is basically a respectable woman. And if she were not so hopeful that her husband's medical practice would soon improve, she would never have become so friendly with these women. For the same reason, her husband permits her to spend days on end with them, frittering their time away with the cards.

Jennie is a handsome, dark-haired woman of about thirty-three. Not very highly educated, but definitely not scatter-brained, either. In America for sixteen years now, she worked twelve of them as a "maid" in other people's homes. But very diligently she saved her money and bought herself a doctor.

How does one do that? Say a girl in such circumstances meets a young tailor or presser whose ambition is to be a doctor. What does he do to get the money for his schooling? He sells himself. There are always plenty of buyers around. There are many older and even younger girls looking to liberate themselves from the sweatshop. Especially for a doctor. To have a doctor for a husband is no trivial thing! Among no other people in the world is the title "Doctor" as highly prized as it is among us Jews. To a Jewish woman the word "doctor" has a more enchanting sound than the sweetest music. Usually the potential "doctor" looks for the girl, since she will work for him and live in secret with him until he graduates. Then they will live together openly.

There was a time when ninety-nine out of a hundred such cases turned out tragically, because the moment the young man finished medical school he realized that, in the first place, his female slave was old and homely, and secondly, he was now in a position to marry an attractive woman with a tidy sum of money. And since they had never been legally married anyway, he simply ditched her without the faintest twinge of compunction. (Where children were born to such couples, the solution, of course, was not that simple.)

Doctor Cyril, whose real name was Shapronovich, had an overwhelming desire to be rid of his young wife, but every once in a while she reminded him that there are such things in this world as vitriol, knives, revolvers, etc. As a physician he grasped her meaning instantly, and knowing that his Jennie was a woman of her word, the poor fellow had to give up every hope of ever becoming a free man.

On this particular occasion, two women are absent from the customary circle because they have besmirched themselves even in the eyes of their tolerant friends. Actually only one of them, Mrs. Cohen, had gone beyond the limit, but since Mrs. Alpert was her closest friend, the world would surely judge her guilty by association. What heinous thing had Mrs. Cohen done? She had merely run away with her own daughter's fiancé and was living with him openly, leaving her husband and children to fend for themselves.

It is no secret that among our women in America card playing is quite the accepted thing. Everybody plays. There are, however, three different classes of players.

The least interesting class consists of women who play occasionally with their husbands, children or close friends.

In some homes card playing is practically a necessity—like bread and tea. People with divergent views on moral and social questions, or with conflicting outlooks on life, come together for the sole purpose of playing cards, In such cases, in order that the company should not become bored or—even worse—quarrelsome, they stick to neutral subjects like the weather or bringing up children.

The second class of women card players is made up of simple, uneducated housewives—very respectable people—who derive great pleasure out of the game itself. That it helps to pass the time is nothing to be sneezed at. Their husbands, occupied with business during all their waking hours, have no objection to this arrangement; quite the contrary, they usually display a keen interest in the proceedings. At least they know where their wives are.

Among these women, the custom is something like this. Several well-to-do housewives get together and draw up a schedule of games for every day of the week (except Sunday) in a different home. During the games they take an agreed upon amount out of each kitty, and then, when there is a sufficient sum, it goes to the hostess, who buys herself an article of clothing or jewelry, as a gift. At the same time, the competitive drive is also satisfied.

The third class consists throughout of shamelessly cynical women to whom the concepts of honor and honesty are "small-townish." Mainly they are ostentatious *nouveaux riches* with varying backgrounds, but they have one thing in common—they are all inveterate gamblers. The most important part of their lives is card playing, by which they win money to pay for their other pleasures. They steal from their husbands, their lovers and each other. They cheat and occasionally are caught using marked cards. They swear falsely, make deadly enemies out of their "best friends."

They are happiest when they can play cards with men, preferably not their husbands. For that reason they love to spend their vacations in the country—"in the mountains"— where they can be free as the birds and play whenever, wherever and with whomever they please. At home they encounter certain difficulties. Their husbands might discover, for ex-

ample, that they are not playing whist or casino or even plain
pinochle for five cents a hundred points, but open poker for
two, three and five dollars a hand. Not to mention their language. If they were to play at home they'd have to keep it
clean, which would take all the fun out of the game. . . .

Sadie Resnick indicated to her friends which seats they
should take. To Fanya she said:

"My pretty little Gypsy, do you have a new pinochle deck
in your house?"

"Sure!" Fanya responded happily. "Here, I have them
ready!"

No one even examined the cards, just to show they trusted
her.

Mrs. Resnick sat down opposite Fanya so she could coach
the beginner. Mrs. LaFontaine was partners with Mrs. Kaplan.
Mrs. Smith and the doctor's wife played two-handed pinochle
at a separate little table.

Sadie had a particular reason for initiating Fanya into her
group. She was determined to make Fanya "one of the girls,"
to make her understand that her husband's ideas and habits
were not sacred, that it wouldn't hurt Manilov's pocketbook
one bit if he hired a servant to help his wife with the house-
work. And if she could persuade her to "have a little fun on
the side," it would serve him right—that pious hypocrite who
goes around boasting about his chaste little wife! Just let his
virtuous little bird once realize how pretty she really is, let
her once experience the sweet excitement of another man's
embrace—then, my angel, he'll be groveling at your feet!

Sadie Resnick felt truly sorry for Fanya. Such a fresh
young creature, in the bloom of life—and she can't do whatever her heart desires. How would she ever learn about life,
locked up in that gilded cage of hers? All day long without a
man nearby, nobody to look at for days at a time!

"What kind of cards are you hiding there under the table,
you French bitch?"

"Since when can you see through a table?"

"Let's play an honest game!"

"Positively—don't we always?"

"Then keep your hands where we can see them!"

"Mind your own goddamn business!"

"Aha!"

"Aha what? You don't scare me, Sadie! Just remember not to trump my kings, or I'll get my boys after your girls!"

"Be careful the same thing doesn't happen to you as happened with the dentist and Mrs. Richman's daughter!"

"What happened with Mrs. Richman's daughter?"

"Nothing special—he just filled her cavity!"

"And she's such a young, innocent girl!"

"Compared to her mother she's a slow learner!"

They played a few hands without commentary until Mrs. LaFontaine announced playfully:

"Hey girls, Sophie just put her queen on top of my jack!"

"Why not? Where is it written that the man always has to be on top?"

They all howled, except Fanya, who blushed more in humiliation than in embarrassment.

"Will you quit looking at my cards!"

"Who's looking? Why don't you keep them closer to your chest?"

"If my chest was as skinny as yours I wouldn't have so much trouble!"

"Why don't you girls shut up and play cards?" complained Mrs. Smith from the other table.

"Oh, you know her, that French-Canadian show-off! She thinks because something pleases her husband she's got to show it to the whole world! First she spreads her legs and then she complains—"

Trying to lighten the growing tension, Mrs. Kaplan sang her favorite ditty as she dealt out the next hand:

> Poker poker let us play!
> I hope your luck ain't tough!
> Lucky women get too much
> Most of us never enough!

"Bravo!"

"Three cheers for Kaplan!"

"Sing it again, Sophie!"

"Hey, Kaplan, what poet taught you those lines?"

"I made it up myself!"

"You don't say! A genius!"

"Listen to them! You might think it's the first time they heard it!"

Sadie Resnick beamed appreciatively at Mrs. Kaplan. Her little song had come just in the nick of time. With songs and jokes like these they would open Fanya's mind, put some sense into it. She herself loved to tell spicy stories during the game, but now, wanting Fanya's undivided attention to the cards, she postponed it until they were finished playing. Then, keeping her eyes on Fanya, she held forth:

"This is a true story, girls. Some of you might even know who I'm talking about. It all started when this friend of mine complained to me that his life was so boring he sometimes felt like leaving his wife and kids and running away. He was a bit of a shnook but I sympathized with him. When I asked him a couple of questions he broke down and told me what was really bothering him. He'd been married for nine years. Up until seven-eight months ago he and his wife had been pretty happy. Then a friend of hers from St. Louis came to visit—a man who'd been madly in love with her when they were both younger. You can imagine what happened.

"From what he was telling me—or maybe it was the way he was telling it—I got the idea that he wanted me to talk to his wife about what she was doing and maybe help them patch things up. As soon as I met her I could see they really were not suited for each other. She was still young, pretty as a rose in June. Next to her he looked like an old man. She told me not to feel so sorry for him. Was he sorry for her when he married her and ruined her young life?

"Well, some time later I noticed that he seemed happier, more lively, almost younger. When I asked him how things were going, he confided to me that his wife had come to realize that a husband is still a man. I couldn't quite figure out what he meant, so I decided to visit his wife again, this time on my own. When I saw her I was almost scared out of my wits. She looked terrible. Like ten years older.

" 'What the hell's wrong with you?' I asked her.

"So she tells me that her niece from St. Louis had come to

New York to marry a friend who had moved here recently. You can guess who that was. Truth is stranger than fiction. Well, her lover and her niece got married, which was bad enough. But then a few weeks after the wedding, damn if he doesn't come and ask her to pick up where they'd left off. She was shocked out of her drawers. What an insult! He tried to convince her: 'Why does it matter to you that I already have a wife? Don't you have a husband?'

"And no matter how hard I tried to explain to her that it wasn't such a bad idea, the foolish woman refused to be talked out of her old-fashioned habits. I argued with her: 'Before, when you wanted to leave your husband, it really was not the right thing to do. We used to do silly things like that in the old days, but not anymore.' You should've heard her bawl. 'He'll never live to see the day, that four-flusher!'

"What do you say to such a greenhorn!"

Although it wasn't the first time they'd heard Sadie Resnick tell the story, or some version of it, they listened with commendable attention, for the sake of the newcomer.

"You've got to be a first-class dummy to pass up an opportunity like that!" commented Mrs. Smith.

"Don't worry," said Mrs. Kaplan. "As she grows older she'll get smarter!"

"Anyway, there's one young man with a healthy appetite, I'll say that for him!" Mrs. Resnick concluded, looking pointedly at Fanya.

"It should only happen to me!" prayed Mrs. LaFontaine.

As they were taking leave of Fanya, Sadie Resnick made sure to coach them: "Well, girls, that was a lovely game of whist we played today, wasn't it!"

"Sure was! Let's do it again soon!"

In this way they agreed among themselves upon the story they would tell their husbands, just in case they should be asked. . . .

5　Right from the start Fanya felt an acute dislike for her guests and their card games. Most of all she was dismayed by their language. In the beginning she was at

least excited by the air of adventure, but it soon palled on her.
And since her husband had arranged the whole thing, he, too,
lost stature in her eyes.

When they began playing for high stakes and Mrs. Resnick launched into her "lectures" on the art of concealing
their losses from their husbands, Fanya could stand it no
longer and reported the entire affair to Moyshe. She expected
him to become angry, to be offended by their behavior, but
after some hesitation he only seemed to grow more and more
confused.

"What are you planning to do about it?" he finally asked.

"You'll see soon enough what I'm planning to do!" she retorted coolly, as if he'd insulted her. Moyshe, however, seemed
not to notice how hurt she was by his attitude. He only grew
prouder of her innocent purity; it was a source of satisfaction
to him that she was repelled by their crude conversation. He'd
better warn Sadie Resnick to curb her tongue in his wife's
presence.

Fanya couldn't make peace with his indifference, his lack
of concern about her feelings. Why didn't he say something?
Why was he afraid to speak up? Suddenly, as if commanded by
some inner voice, she was extremely displeased with her husband. When he put his arms around her she almost shuddered
in loathing. It was just like the vulgar talk of those women.
Were they his friends? Full of suspicion, she pushed him away.

Those stories told by her new acquaintances—they perplexed her so much, yet she was dimly aware of some sort of
salaciousness arising within her own soul. She kept imagining Mrs. Resnick, Mrs. LaFontaine and Mrs. Kaplan in the
arms of their lovers. . . . Where did Moyshe fit into all this? It
struck her that Yudin was a much handsomer and much more
interesting man than her husband. If she had married him she
would now be infinitely happier.

These thoughts filled her with guilt, then shame, as if
someone had deliberately humiliated her. She grew furious
with herself, her hands and face felt as if they were stained
with an indelible substance that she could not wash off.

Finally she made up her mind: she would get rid of those
women once and for all, and the sooner the better. She could

no longer even bear to think about them. Not once had they asked her opinion about anything, not even as to when they could use her home again. They made all the decisions themselves, as if she were only a child. She'd show them—she wasn't the *nebekhl* they took her for. They couldn't push her around this way any longer.

So one day, a little while before they were due to arrive, she left the house. Not knowing where else to go, she found herself on the way to Moyshe's store. Just as she was descending the stairs from the El train, she caught sight of Mrs. Resnick and the others climbing the stairs to the opposite platform, on their way to her house. Her heart leaped for joy. Now perhaps they would realize that she couldn't stand them, that she didn't want them in her home, that she would be happy never to see them again.

Out of her whole jarring experience with them, only two things remained vivid with her: a dark suspicion of their motives and a genuine sympathy for the woman Mrs. Resnick had told them about that first day. If she knew who that woman was and where she lived, she'd go straight to her and tell her how wisely she had acted.

As she turned the corner toward Moyshe's store she heard her name called. She looked up. Striding toward her energetically was Yudin.

"Well, well, how nice to see you, Mrs. Manilov! You're on your way to Moyshe's? I'm just coming from there—it's so busy I couldn't even talk to him—"

Consternation overwhelmed her. She couldn't utter a sound. She felt as if he had been following her, that he knew every step she took, every thought she had. Otherwise, how explain his presence there at that precise moment? Did it have anything to do with Mrs. Resnick? No, that was silly! How could Mrs. Resnick have known that she'd leave her house today, of all days? But why was Yudin telling her about Moyshe's store? Was he giving her a message not to go there now? Why didn't he say something else? Why didn't *she* say something?

"How did you happen to be at Moyshe's today?" she heard herself asking him. Why had she said that, anyway? What business was it of hers? She had spoken so seriously, however—all the while keeping her eyes down—that Yudin took encouragement from it.

"I made a special trip there today, Mrs. Manilov, hoping you'd be there. . . . Let's walk a bit—"

He took her arm to guide her across the heavily trafficked street. Fanya thanked him politely and let herself be led. Why not spend a half hour with him before she went to the store? After all, she couldn't insult her husband's best friend.

As they turned into Broadway, Yudin suddenly became loquacious. "Whenever I think about this world we live in, I'm always amazed how miraculous it is! It was only yesterday that Manilov and I were 'riding horses'—him on a broken shovel and me on a crooked old cane. We used to gallop down to the river to swim. We'd take off our clothes, hang them up on sticks that were hammered into the soft sand, and before we jumped into the cold water we'd bet three buttons or ten cherry pits on who could turn a somersault in the water first."

He spoke so naturally, with so much enthusiasm, that Fanya somehow felt refreshed. Every shadow of suspicion fell away from her. Her spirits rose, her head cleared, and she laughed from the depths of her soul. All at once she felt free, bright, joyful, as if she'd been suddenly revitalized.

"Well, which one of you used to win?" she asked.

"Usually it was me!" he laughed.

"You know, Mr. Yudin, I think the best time of our life is when we're young. . . ." She sounded as if she really believed she was the first person who'd ever uttered that sentiment.

Yudin smiled in agreement and added: "It would be even better if people never grew older. . . ."

"You mean we should die in our youth?"

"Who said anything about dying? Why couldn't we always stay young and healthy?"

"How is that possible?" she asked naively.

"It isn't, but to a certain extent, people can make it happen."

She looked at him questioningly. He seemed to be trying to tell her something, but so far his meaning was eluding her.

Yudin continued to philosophize. "If we all have to die, if

life is no more than a dream, a fairy tale, why can't we at least try to stay young, healthy and cheerful? Why can't we think only about living and nothing else? Only about life, life, life—live and enjoy living, in full measure! I hope you understand me, Mrs.—" He hesitated, "Mrs. Manilov."

Her eyes glowed. Yes, he was really a much more interesting man than Moyshe! And what he was saying was absolutely true. And the way he said it, the words he used—never before in her life had she heard such beautiful, fascinating words. . . .

Engrossed in conversation, they had walked much farther than Fanya had planned. Could this possibly be 42nd Street already?

They both laughed at the same time.

"You know something, Mrs. Manilov, all this walking and talking has made me hungry for lunch!"

Fanya smiled.

"Are you laughing at me, Mrs. Manilov? You're thinking I always have food on my mind?"

"No, not that."

"What are you smiling at, then?"

"Your remark reminded me that we're all human and we all have to eat."

"I don't understand—"

"I haven't even had breakfast yet—" Instantly she regretted her words. What business was it of his that she hadn't eaten?

"For goodness' sake!" he exclaimed. "Why didn't you say so? Let's go into this cafeteria."

"No, thank you."

"Why not?"

"I don't like to eat there."

"But if you're hungry?"

"It's all right, I won't die of starvation."

"Tell you what, Mrs. Manilov. I'll just stop into this grocery here and pick up something." He turned, but she put her hand on his arm.

"Thank you, but please don't! I can't eat out in the middle of the street."

"Then let me take you home—"

"Home? But I was on my way to the store. Well—all right—thank you—"

The El train was so crowded they barely had room to stand. And since the passengers entering and leaving had to push their way through, it was natural for Yudin to protect Fanya by putting his arm around her waist. She was certain he was doing it for that reason alone, but it seemed to her that each time he did so he left his arm there a moment longer. The blood rushed to her face, but she said nothing.

As they entered the apartment, Fanya picked up an apple from the table and bit into it ravenously.

Without a word, Yudin went into the kitchen, found eggs, put up some milk on the stove, and before Fanya realized what he was doing, he was serving her scrambled eggs and a cup of warm milk. She practically shouted in astonishment:

"What an unusual man you are, Yudin!"

He grinned. "Lunch is served, Madame!"

"You eat something, too, Mr. Yudin, I've already taken the edge off my hunger."

"No, no, this is all for you—"

"There's enough here for both of us!"

She put on the teakettle and brought bread and butter to the table.

As he ate, Yudin kept his eyes fixed on Fanya's face, which turned rosier and rosier.

"Mrs. Manilov, I've just come to an interesting philosophical conclusion—"

"What's that, Yudin?"

"I've discovered that after you eat, you're no longer hungry!"

Fanya laughed out loud. Looking fondly at Yudin, she stood up to get the tea, but he had anticipated her and was in the kitchen before she could take a step. As he came back with two glasses of tea, Fanya said:

"You think you have to earn the right to eat?"

"Why should I be any more privileged than you?"

"You're a marvelous guest!" Again she regretted her almost involuntary words. Why was she talking to him like this? His way of speaking, his solicitous behavior, moved her so deeply that she couldn't help showing her admiration. She understood—she sensed rather than understood it—that this should not be happening. She felt as if she were somehow committing a great wrong against someone.

"I have two requests of you, Mrs. Manilov," he said, breaking into her thoughts.

"Yes?"

"First, let me clean up here, and second, please allow me to light up a cigar. . . ."

"With pleasure! But there really isn't much to clean up."

"All right, then if you do it, I'll smoke my cigar, and when you're finished we'll chat awhile."

Fanya looked at him gratefully. For the first time in her life a man—and an educated man at that—had spoken to her as if she were his equal, a person able to understand things as he did.

"I don't know how to say this, Mrs. Manilov, but sometimes I feel like being so brazen, so audacious, that I want to swallow all of life at one gulp. As long as I'm already living, let me enjoy it, let life rage and storm like a volcano! At such moments I can't help thinking of those unfortunate people who are driven to taking their own lives. I always ask myself: Why do they do it? What more do they want out of life than life itself—good or bad—so long as they're alive? Things are not working out for them? So what? They're alive—so much to the good! You understand what I'm trying to say, Mrs. Manilov? I think that anyone who really wants to can make his life more interesting, more beautiful, more worthwhile. Financial position? Well, we all have to think about that seriously, of course. If you've got money—fine! If not, it's not the end of the world. We only live once in this world, and if you don't take advantage of it, you'll never get another chance. What happens in the next world, nobody has ever come back to tell us! I hope you understand me, Mrs. Manilov."

All the time he was talking, Fanya stood by the table holding two glasses she had picked up to take into the kitchen.

When he had finished, she put them back on the table like an automaton and stood motionless, intoxicated by a stream of thoughts and emotions. Though she hadn't understood some of the words he used, she grasped the full import of what he said, and a bright light burst into her life. She sensed something very significant happening within her, although there were as yet no outward signs of it.

Suddenly, almost magically, she felt older than her years, as if she had lived an entire lifetime. No longer was she a helpless young woman, dependent on someone else. She was a complete individual, responsible for everything she did, every step she took.

Yudin leaned back in his chair, staring at the cigar smoke as it curled upward in tiny gray ringlets, rising higher and higher above his head like a circular column. He, too, had been powerfully affected by his words. He was only now recalling what he had said, and only now did he comprehend their real significance. Emotionally drained, he realized that life can be a terribly difficult struggle and that some individuals, unable to bear the heavy burden, might easily be tempted to get out from under it.

Deep in their own thoughts, neither he nor Fanya had noticed that the day was dying. The apartment drew darker and darker. Sudden light stabbed at Yudin's eyes. Startled, he looked around for its source, but it was the lights going on in the windows across the street.

"Oh! Is it that late already?" He leaped up from his chair. "Time for me to go!"

"Yes!" Fanya exclaimed, not even knowing what question she was responding to.

As Yudin shook hands with her, he avoided her eyes. It seemed to her that he had been crying.

He understood why she did not ask him to come visit her again. He knew with every nerve in his body that no matter when he came, Fanya would be happy to see him. . . .

Stepping into the kitchen, Fanya lit two burners on the stove, but did not put any pots on them. For several minutes she stood there absently, then told herself she'd better prepare supper.

She quickly changed her clothes, returned to the kitchen and put the pots on a low flame. Then she lay down on a sofa in the dining room.

"*I made a special trip, hoping you'd be there,*" he had said. She was a little bit hurt by that. It couldn't have been true. How would he have known that she would go to the store that day, of all days? What should she have said? She didn't know exactly, but she shouldn't have let it pass. It wasn't very nice of him. . . .

She turned over on her side and dozed off, pressing a small pillow to her heart. What was wrong with her? As soon as she closed her eyes she started dreaming she was laughing and woke herself up. What was so funny? Her face turned crimson. Never again would she let herself be maneuvered into Mrs. Resnick's company. And certainly she would never let Yudin put his arm around her, as he had done on the train. . . .

After she served Moyshe his supper she went straight to bed. Her behavior disturbed him. What could it signify? Why hadn't she eaten with him? Didn't she feel well? Anyway, was that a reason for leaving him alone at the table without an explanation? He grew more and more resentful, but said nothing.

When he left the house the next morning he was visibly upset, but Fanya pretended not to notice. She lay abed late, her eyes open but unseeing. She felt herself changing, heart and soul, into a different person. Somehow she was becoming more masculine, more independent, more complete. And the more confident and complete she grew, the more indifferent she felt toward Moyshe. And the greater this indifference, the clearer and brighter and happier she herself became.

"*As long as I'm already living, let me enjoy life, let it rage and storm like a volcano!*"

Recalling the words, Fanya felt a surge of strength suffuse her limbs. She threw off the covers, stretched pleasurably, and gazed for a few seconds at her half-naked body, from which came a hot, fresh scent. She sprang out of bed, skipped into the kitchen, prepared a big breakfast, and enjoyed every bite. Humming and singing, she danced through her household chores. There was nothing in the world she wanted more at this moment than for Yudin to walk through the door. She would greet him so warmly he would shout for joy.

Standing before the mirror, she imagined him putting his arms around her. She smiled admiringly at her own strong white arms. Yudin would soon be arriving. She had no doubt about it. That's what she wanted, and that's what would happen!

She started singing again, one song after another. The more she sang, the more intoxicated she became with the sound of her own voice; the more fiercely life pulsated in her veins, the more powerfully surged the sources of her passion.

"To live, to live, to swallow all of life in one gulp!"

She pirouetted around the room, waving her arms, kicking up her legs. Her long braids came apart over her shoulders, her eyes blazed with glowing sparks of life. Her breath was a flame that cut the air like a white-hot blade.

Little by little she sobered up. When the storm had passed completely she felt fatigued, bone-weary, drained of energy, like a surgical patient whose anesthetic has begun to wear off. She lay down on the sofa and slept soundly until dusk.

Moyshe was too proud to let the matter rest, but he did not wish to quarrel with Fanya, either. He decided to ease the tension by inviting Yudin to come home with him the next evening.

"I've brought a guest, Fanyetchke. I've asked him to visit us more often, but he keeps making excuses. Maybe he wants you to send him a special invitation. . . ."

"I'm always glad to have company—but why a special invitation?"

Moyshe seemed pleased enough with her answer. The mood changed. They joked a lot, ate a lot, drank more than usual, talked more than usual. Especially Fanya. Overcoming her surprise, she was so happy with the world that evening that her joy sang out of her with every gesture, every movement of her body.

After supper Moyshe had another surprise for her. He took out of his pocket a deck of expensive playing cards and handed them to Fanya.

"Play a few games of casino with Yudin, but don't disgrace me, please! I've been bragging to him that you can now play better than me. Don't disappoint me! But be careful, Fanya, he's an expert!"

"Yes, I've heard he's a wonderful player," she said politely, her tone almost betraying her.

Yudin gazed at her affectionately until she looked up at him, then he lowered his eyes.

"I think you should know, however, that I play for high stakes. . . ."

"How much?"

"A penny a point. . . ."

Fanya laughed a bit too heartily.

"All right, Mama, play for whatever stakes he likes—here's your bankroll!" Moyshe took a handful of silver out of his pocket and pushed it across the table.

Fanya and Yudin sat down at one end of the table while Moyshe, at the other end, turned his attention to his accounts.

They talked and laughed and Moyshe kept making one mistake after another in his addition. Finally he excused himself and moved to the parlor with his books.

"He doesn't know anything?" Yudin asked as soon as Moyshe was out of earshot.

"About what?"

"You told him nothing?" Yudin insisted.

"Nothing."

"Good, good! You did the right thing."

Fanya stared at him in amazement.

"I thought I'd go mad!"

"Over what? What are you talking about, Yudin?"

"Women are supposed to be more intuitive than men about these things. . . ."

Through her confusion, Fanya began to admit something to herself. She blushed, played a card.

He did not take his eyes off her face, but said nothing.

From the moment he asked her whether Moyshe "knew anything" and she answered no, Fanya realized that their relationship had grown a bit too intimate. She wasn't even as surprised by his question as she had acted, although she was not sure why she hadn't told her husband anything yet. She was treating him unfairly perhaps, but what was she guilty of? Still, at the very earliest opportunity—

"You should have taken in the black ten with your good ten right away," Yudin said softly.

"How did you know I had a good ten?"

"Because I don't have it and this is the last hand."

He was obviously correct, but she didn't feel like admitting it. She kept silent. Better pay more attention to the cards, she cautioned herself.

"I'm afraid this game is mine," he apologized.

"It's not over yet!"

"Would you like to bet, Mrs. Manilov?"

"Any time you say, Mr. Yudin!" There was a note in her voice that surprised her as she heard it.

"How much, Mrs. Manilov?"

"Anything you say."

"I'll take your word for it. . . ."

In the next deal, after winning a few points, she clapped her hands, gleeful as a child.

"It's too soon to count your chickens, Mrs. Manilov."

"Won't that be big news!" she teased. "Mr. Yudin, the champion card player of the Bronx, loses to an amateur! I wonder how much I should bet you?"

"Go as high as you dare—I'll pay up without asking any questions."

"Remember that!"

"You, too, Mrs. Manilov. . . ."

They concentrated a bit more on their cards, yet Yudin, the more experienced player, came close to losing a game that was almost predetermined by the cards themselves.

After they totaled up the score, she sat calmly, smiling to herself. Her eyes stayed tenderly on Yudin's face. What would he demand of her, now that he had won the bet? A myriad of thoughts and feelings raced through her heart and brain, but it was beyond her ability to put them together or sort them out. She was just as content to leave it to fate. Whatever was destined to happen would happen—and soon.

Yudin took a cigar out of his pocket, fiddled with it for a while before he lit it. When he finally spoke, it was on a subject having nothing to do with cards. For the rest of the evening he avoided that topic altogether. Realizing what he was doing, Fanya thought all the more highly of him for it: aside from being an expert player he was also a gentleman. Sooner or later he would demand his winnings, but no matter what happened later, he was silent about it now, and that was the correct way for a gentleman to behave.

As Yudin said good night to his hosts, Moyshe apologized for being too busy to play. Yudin replied that he had spent a pleasant evening and enjoyed Fanya's cooking, and since Moyshe had taken advantage of the opportunity to take care of business, everybody had come out a winner.

"And who won the game, Fanya?" Moyshe remembered to ask after Yudin had left.

"He's very good, your friend. . . ." she blushed, walking into the kitchen "for a glass of water."

It was daybreak before she fell asleep.

All night long she thought about him. His self-confidence was contagious. It gave him a taller, stronger appearance than he actually had. His gentle way of speaking, his considerate behavior when he won the game—that's what made him so captivating. But deep inside her she knew that all these virtues she saw in him were not the essential thing. They helped to salve her conscience, but she was becoming aware of something much more elemental. It frightened her and delighted her at the same time. . . .

6   The following morning, when Moyshe went off to business, Fanya felt a sense of relief. His presence disturbed her thoughts, made her uncomfortable. With him out of the house, she could do some clear thinking. She was certain that Yudin would soon be arriving—something she wanted very much to happen—but just as strong was her hope that he not come at all. What good would it do? How would it all end?

No, the situation was no good. Worse, it was ugly. The thought that she had fallen in love with him made her face flame. It could lead to nothing but trouble, the kind of trouble from which she should flee as from a conflagration. What would Moyshe do if he ever found out? But what was there for him to find out? She had not stopped loving him. On the contrary, she loved him even more. And he was crazy about her. Whatever she wanted, he bought for her. If nothing else, she owed him her respect. If she were really a decent woman she wouldn't even be at home when Yudin arrived. That's what she should do—get away from here at once!

She dressed quickly, ran out the door. She would ride downtown to Moyshe's store. No, first she would walk until she felt tired, then she would take the train. Out here she would be able to think more clearly than in the crowded car where people jostled you from all sides.

She walked rapidly, without being conscious of doing so, and thought about her life with Moyshe. But Yudin's image kept interfering. She drove it away. She must forget him, forget even what he looked like. Moyshe was her husband. Yudin was a total stranger. She knew nothing about him, about his family. She wasn't like Mrs. Resnick or Mrs. Kaplan or those others. She was a respectable married woman. In all fairness she should tell Moyshe everything and promise him it wouldn't happen again. No, that was silly! Tell him what? Nothing had happened that she could tell him about. It would all sound so childish. . . .

When her legs grew tired and her gait slowed, her thoughts became more lucid. Why was she going to Moyshe's store now? What reason would she give for going there? They had agreed she wouldn't come to the store anymore. Moyshe had told her: when the boss's wife comes to the place of business too often the employees lose respect for her. He was right, too. She recalled how they had annoyed her. So what reason would she have for coming there today? She didn't want to stay home alone? Why not, all of a sudden? Because Yudin was coming? What would that mean? In the first place, how did she know he was coming? And if he did, what of it?

No, she could not go to the store now. She'd better just walk around a little longer, then she'd go back and lock herself in the apartment. She wouldn't open the door to anyone until Moyshe came home.

She turned around and started back the same way she had come. She must think about her husband, only of her husband. As if to spite her, however, images of Sadie Resnick and her friends arose in her mind. She remembered their words, she thought about them, and only now did she begin to understand their real meaning. And remarkably, she was not ashamed of thinking about them, nor did she feel in her heart any of her previous resentment. Those women must have had many lovers. The thought seemed to give her some strange satisfaction. She would very much like to know if their husbands were aware of what was going on, and what they said about it if they knew. Does Moyshe know about these "other men" his friends boasted about? Of course he knows. He must. Now she was beginning to see the whole picture. Otherwise, why would he have told her he wouldn't exchange one of her footsteps for a thousand Sadie Resnicks?

As she put her key in the door a neighbor told her that soon after she had left the apartment a man had come calling, a "swell-dressed" handsome gentleman. He had rung the doorbell a long time, first down below and then upstairs, too.

From her description it could only have been Yudin. Fanya grew nervous. She entered the apartment, forgetting to shut the door behind her, and fell onto the sofa without even taking off her coat. The house was dark, but she did not turn on any lights. She lay on the sofa thinking about Mrs. Resnick and her friends. She created mental pictures of them giving themselves to their men. She heard their words again and to her great surprise found herself agreeing with many of the ideas they had expressed.

Feeling a sudden draft of cold air, she got up to see where it was coming from. Yes, no wonder—she had neglected to shut the door. She turned on the lights, closed the door, strode angrily around the room. Tonight she would not cook supper. They would eat delicatessen—she had plenty of that in the icebox. As she paced back and forth, her thoughts went round and round and ended up in the same place. She felt insulted, degraded, resentful and finally could not restrain her tears. She wept as if she were deriving a special kind of pleasure from it.

The doorbell. It must be Moyshe. She let him in.

"What's wrong?" he exclaimed in alarm.

"Everything's wrong! Why did you ever introduce me to Mrs. Resnick and her gang? Why? Why?"

"What's wrong, for God's sake? What happened?"

"They talked about such vulgar things—and now I can't get their words out of my head!"

Surprised and concerned, Moyshe did not know how to answer her. Instead, he kissed her, caressed her, tried every way he could think of to soothe her. His tenderness only seemed to make things worse, but he continued his efforts to calm her.

Suddenly Fanya threw herself at him, kissing him wildly, biting his lips, his neck. She tore her clothes off. . . .

As she lay clasped in her husband's arms she felt an overpowering urge to cry out "Yudin! Yudin!" But a still stronger force restrained her. Burrowing into Moyshe's chest, she screamed:

"Choke me! Beat me! Tear me into bits!"

Before he left for work in the morning, Moyshe kissed her fervently, embraced her, whispered endearments. But she could not find a word to say in response, as if she had done him a great favor by allowing him to touch her. Yet when he had gone, she was full of remorse. She tried to direct her thoughts only to him—kind thoughts, tender thoughts, like in the old days. He worked so hard, day and night, and who was he doing it all for, if not for her? Everything he owned was as much hers as it was his. Never once had he complained about how much she spent on herself. All these and other virtues she found in her husband, yet the more good qualities she found in him the more disconnected she felt from him and the farther away he receded. None of it was true. Moyshe wasn't the man she was trying to persuade herself he was. Without too much effort she could recall just as many distasteful things about him. . . .

Soon she detected a feeling toward him which was neither hostile nor sympathetic—it was merely indifferent. As soon as she realized this she again started checking off all his virtues, but now they all seemed absurd. Whatever he had done, he had done because he had no other choice.

Why didn't she care about him any longer? If Moyshe were to die today, would she cry? No, she wouldn't. She would observe the seven days of mourning, Yudin would come to console her—and stay the night. Even if he wanted to leave, she wouldn't let him. The two of them—just the two of them—all alone, with no one to interrupt them. . . .

But suppose Yudin was angry with her? He might be. He must have understood that she left the house deliberately. She shouldn't have done that. He would think she was avoiding him because she was afraid he would demand payment of the bet. No, she should not have gone out. If only he would come in now, she'd say to him:

"Mr. Yudin, tell me what I owe you. Let's settle up." No doubt he could use the money, little as it was. His only income came from the English lessons he gave to immigrants.

God, how passionately he had looked at her! And he was always looking at her—she had noticed that. Who else had noticed it? But why did he always turn his eyes away when she looked at him? No, she shouldn't have gone out—it was not a nice thing to do, not nice at all. She must tell him how sorry she was she had done that. She had such warm and tender feelings for him. Why didn't he come back?

She got out of bed, put on her robe and went into the kitchen to make herself some cocoa. The sudden clamor of the doorbell almost knocked the cup out of her hand. Before she could press the buzzer, someone was already at the upstairs door.

"Who is it?"

No response.

"Who's there?" she cried in frightened anticipation.

"It's me!"

Happily she opened the door and ran back into the bedroom to get dressed.

"I was just thinking about you!" she called from the bedroom and was instantly sorry she'd said it. She must be insane!

"Sit down, Mr. Yudin, I'll be right out!"

How wretched he looked! How lonely! A deep surge of pity brought tears to her eyes. What could she do to comfort him, what could she say? If she could only think of one kind word! But her tongue refused to move. Did he know how he was tormenting her by looking at her this way? What could she do to ease his pain?

He came closer, took her hand. "Forgive me, Fanyetchka! I couldn't stay away. But I can't bear my great misfortune—"

"What misfortune?" she asked apprehensively.

"I'm dying for love of you, Fanyetchka, and I know how hopeless it is. Forgive me, Fanya, I'm not worthy of you—"

What was happening to her? How had they gotten over to the sofa? Why was she sitting on his lap? He was kissing her lips, her throat, her eyes. His arms were tightening around her. Her face was on fire. Why were there tears in his eyes?

"What shall I do, Fanyetchka, what shall I do?"

"It's all right, it's all right. . . ."

Her heart trembled as if a strong wind were trying to rip it out of her body.

But Yudin's voice—it penetrated her soul, entered every little cell of her body. She was so happy now, so happy. Hold me closer, closer, Yudin my beloved, my only friend. . . .

With a chaste smile on her beautiful lips, a smile full of love and contentment, she nestled in his arms, surrendering herself to him completely. . . .

Fanyetchka, Fanyetchka, my whole life is in your hands, in your hands, my dearest. . . .

Fanya still does not comprehend what happened. Some powerful force has struck her, sent her soaring higher, higher, and nothing in the world can now stop her flight. . . .

Women

SURROUNDED BY high, thick woods, as though designed that way to prevent strangers from prying, sprawls the ancient city of Pereyaslav.

At its right, and connected to the city by a short wooden bridge, lies the suburb called "the Pidvorki."

Pereyaslav itself, with its long, narrow, muddy streets, with its houses leaning against each other like headstones in a graveyard, with its dilapidated, consumptive-looking gray walls and its broken windowpanes stuffed with rags—this town of Pereyaslav is not so much different from other places inhabited by Jews. Here, too, you withered and faded even before you had a chance to bloom; here, too, even before the rose opened its pale eyelids, even before the human eye could grow large with wonderment about life's mysteries, the sated worm was already poised on your listless body, greeting you with a venomous smirk. . . .

Here, too, people existed on miracles. Here, too, they were fruitful and multiplied without any rhyme, reason or purpose. Here, too, people talked about earning a livelihood, about enjoying riches and pleasures, about better days to come, and they did this with the same kind of outward faith and the same kind of inner disbelief that one feels while reading aloud legendary tales from venerated books. And they really accepted the notion that all those words were written down somewhere, but that's as far as it went. Not only did they have no conception of the real meaning behind the words, but some of them, having long since given up any hope of ever earning a living, no longer saw any point in wasting their brainpower on such futile efforts.

Evenings, a cloudy blue-gray sky, lachrymose and gloomy, descended upon the city. For the inhabitants of Pereyaslav, however, the darkness was a relief. Weary and disheartened, old before their time, they found some solace in the lap of the unknowable, dreamy, impenetrable night. Their wretchedness receded from them along with their pain and suffering. A mysterious, opaque force concealed everything from them as with a solid stone wall, so that they saw and heard nothing.

They did not hear the feeble cries—plaintive as the mewing of blind kittens—of their languishing children who, as though to spite them, kept asking for food all day long. Nor did they hear the sighing and groaning of their friends and family, who, with the hoarse, complaining tones of a cracked instrument, split the air around them. In their sleep they did not see the starvation-death which fluttered and quivered all around them, suspended on spider webs above their heads.

They did not even notice the spent little fires which fevered tremulously in their own crowded hovels, testifying by their flickering that here lived human beings who still breathed.

Yes, the night was their best time. The mute stillness rocked everyting to sleep, extinguished everything, made forgetting easier.

As soon, however, as the eastern sky caught fire and the flame began to spread, then the first glowing spears fell upon the aching hearts of the people below and set them ablaze. At that moment the air was ripped and shattered by the unstifled hunger-cries of hundreds of children; by desperate calls for help; by lamentations, oaths, curses and maledictions.

A long, continuous imprecation, like a mammoth skein, rolled from house to house, from door to door, from mouth to mouth. People began to stir, walk, run. Half-dressed, their limbs emaciated and their skin all shriveled, their deeply sunken eyes smoldering like hot coals, they crawled and climbed all over each other like worms, tearing the last bites out of each other's mouths, their lips white with poisonous froth.

Yet now they feel bold, free, more spirited. Despite everything, it is summertime. To be sure, they are still smothered and choking, they still lack air to breathe, they are still wasting away from heat and exhaustion. But they now can do without some other life-sustaining necessities. For weeks they can live without firewood—the cooler it is, the better. And the nights are short—you don't need much kerosene for the lamps.

Winter, however, is another story. The skies are angry, sullen. The sun is enervated, the day sick, the frost burns and bites.

People change, too. They become unrecognizable. Forever worried, irritable, downcast, enchained by a grim hopelessness, without the strength even to tear the food out of each other's mouths.

The days are soundless months, the nights interminable years, and the weeks—oh, the weeks!—are eternities.

No one in the world cares about their misery, their loneliness, their cold, hungry lives. Only one companion helps them weep and sigh—the obsessed, desolate, grieving wind, which tears at the flimsy rooftops of their homes and hoots into their cold chimneys like another Cain, condemned by Almighty God to everlasting prowling, wandering, homelessness. . . .

The one bright star in this dark abyss, their pride and their consolation, is the Pidvorki. To support a cantor, a public bathhouse, a burial society, a small home for the aged, several rabbis, to give Sabbath bread to the needy or matzos for Passover to the poor; to provide the dowry for an impoverished Jewish bride, or simply to give alms to a beggar—for all of this the *Pidvorki women* contribute with an open hand. The idle and the sick, the poor and the inconsolable, all found support and protection in the Pidvorki; it was an inexhaustible well that never refused to help anyone. So that for hundreds of miles around, husbands instructed their wives to "take a lesson from the Pidvorki" and they, too, would be happy and prosperous.

It was not in the Pidvorki's high, verdant, velvety hills and broad, flower-sprinkled gardens that they took pride. Nor was it the spacious fields brimming over with cornstalks that bowed gratefully whenever the sun poured down its gold upon them or when a frisky breeze came along and played with them. Nor was it even the clear, translucent river that encircled the Pidvorki, a river in which the sky bathed all day long and you could not tell which was bluer, the water or the sky.

All these things matter little to them. Perhaps they don't even know such things exist or don't want to know. Whoever bothers his head about such nonsense has thereby become a sinner. They are not Jewish concerns, are they? A big city full of people, with a God over them, with commandments and punishments, with a world-to-come and a wife-and-children in this one! You'd have to be senile to spend your precious time staring at the sky, the fields, the river or other such foolishness which it is demeaning for an older person even to talk about.

No. What they are proudest of—what they boast about—is the Pidvorki women. Not that the Pidvorki women are better looking or taller or more intelligent than other women. They, too, become pregnant every year and bring forth a child, in accordance with the old Jewish custom. Nor is it that they are any more highly esteemed by their husbands. On the contrary, they are treated a hundred times more shabbily than other wives—and that, in truth, is what distinguishes them. Like all other wives, they tolerate the insults and indignities of their husbands without protest.

And yet they are an exception. They are as different from all other wives as the rushing waters of the indefatigable Dnieper are different from a stagnant, moss-covered swamp.

Five o'clock in the morning, while the men are just turning over on the other side and burying their faces in the downy white pillows, all the while emitting strange, fitful noises from their ridiculous red noses, their wives have already put in a half-day's work in the marketplace. Dressed in their light jackets and big blue aprons, on the underside of which hang leather pockets for holding money and making change, they work hard in all sorts of little shops and stalls, weighing and measuring, buying and selling—and they do it all with amazing quickness and dexterity.

Here is one of them in her stall, persuading a barefoot young peasant woman to buy the piece of calico, although the customer actually would rather have the red gingham with the white flowers. She swears that she wouldn't sell this goods to anyone else at twice the price. But suddenly she notices that two of the other marketwomen are following a farmer's wagon. She doesn't really know what's in the wagon, but she leaves her customer and runs after the wagon, too, because the peasant is sure to need axle grease or salt, and a sale like that would be as good as finding ten kopeks in the street. And she is certain that the customer will wait in the stall until she returns, so enchanted is she by the marketwoman's words.

The wagon is already encircled by a score of women, each one trying to outshout the other, each one touting her own wares or reminding the peasant that he and she have done business before. In the midst of the mounting tumult a new clamor is heard—"Chickens, women, chickens! Cheap as dirt!" A nearby landowner has sent out his agent to dispose of his surplus hens. the marketwomen surge toward the chickens, still holding on to the peasant's cart with one hand, until it appears they are going to drag the cart after them, horses and all. For a few hectic minutes they bargain with the agent, advising him not to be so obstinate, to accept their offer, or else he'll only regret it later.

Suddenly there is a new outcry—"*Market-wagons!*"— and the women rush at the wagons of fresh vegetables as if their lives depended on getting there first. They elbow each other, their eyes glistening. Each one would like to corner the whole vegetable market for that day. There is a shrieking and a scolding until finally one or two of them buy up the entire load and the battle is over.

Only then does our marketwoman remember that she has left a customer waiting in her stall. She runs in with a beaming smile and reassures her: since she waited so patiently for such a long time, she can have the very finest piece of red gingham in the shop for even less than the calico. . . .

At eight o'clock, after the farmers have all brought their wagons to market, after the women have finished filling the containers left by their customers, they count up the day's receipts. Each one takes off a certain sum for her own secret little cache—a human being is only flesh and blood, after all, and you never know when you'll need an extra penny, so why fight with your husband every time you need it.

When they have nothing more to do in the shops or stalls, they come together in groups, and each woman tells about some particular incident, some notable feat of the day. They forget all about the curses and insults they hurled at each other in the heat of battle. Long ago they learned that "business is business" and one never bears a grudge against a competitor over that. . . .

Each one speaks with fervor. Deep in her tired, black-ringed eyes burns a tiny, proud flame as she relates the way she got the better of this or that customer, or how she sold something she had already relegated to the scrap heap, and even got a good price for it.

A thin, quavering voice is heard above the others.

"Listen to this! This morning I got up when God Himself was still asleep—"

"You mustn't say such things, Sheyne!"

"So what happened?" other voices urge her on.

"I got out of bed and tiptoed out of the room, so as not to wake anybody up, because Lazer went to bed very late last night—some kind of important meeting at the rabbi's. . . . It was so early that I didn't even want to wake Sarah, who always gets up when I do—it won't hurt her to learn some good habits from her mother. Anyway, at half-past seven, when I saw that no more market-wagons were coming in, I went back to the house to see what was doing there, and as I came in I heard Lazer calling me like he was trying to wake me up. So I went into the bedroom and lay down on the bed and pretended to be asleep. He ran into the room and shook me:

'Wake up, you'll be late for the market!' It was so funny I was afraid I'd burst out laughing, so I sat up and said, '*Oy vey!* Why didn't you wake me up sooner?'"

They all laugh with her, a bright, gentle, contented laughter.

"One morning," says another, "when my husband started waking me, I told him I wouldn't go to the market that day, that it wouldn't hurt him to go himself once in a while!"

This extraordinary notion apparently pleases them tremendously, because they laugh even more heartily. . . .

When the talk gets around to their daughters, however, they grow more serious. Each one tries to reckon up her child's age and asks for help from the others in recalling the exact date her daughter was born, so there will be no miscalculation.

One mother whose daughter has just reached sixteen speaks with a heavy heart. The situation is quite critical. A girl of that age should have a husband. And in this instance there is nothing to prevent it, if only the proper suitor would appear. Her dowry is large enough—a young man who doesn't demand a substantial dowry, who knows what kind of husband he will make? A means of livelihood she will also have —we'll open a little stall for her in the marketplace; she certainly knows how to manage one. The main thing is that God should only send us a young man from a respectable family, so my husband won't blush in shame whenever anyone asks him about his in-laws.

And actually, this is what they all do. When their daughters approach the age of sixteen, suitable husbands are found for them. At the age of twenty they are already "old," mature, worldlywise—they know all about teething, chicken pox, measles, even the croup. Should a child of one of these young mothers fall ill, she will immediately go see a friend who knows more about such things, having already been married two or three years. With the attitude of a consulting physician the friend will ask a series of questions—whether the swellings in the neck are getting larger or smaller, whether they are moving from one part of the neck to another. If so, there's nothing to worry about, it isn't serious. but if they stay in one place, God forbid, she is not to waste another minute and rush the child to the doctor without fail. . . .

As soon as the women finish with the subject of earning a living they move to *yikhus*, a matter dear to the heart of each one of them.

That their children, particularly their daughters, are chaste; that none of them—may we never hear of such things in our town, God forbid, as we do in other places—had ever given birth to a bastard, this is for them the highest degree of well-being and achievement. It makes up for the fact that never in their lives do they hear a word of praise from their husbands and it helps them put up with their own super-human labors.

When they talk of such things, especially when they can toss in a phrase like "the apple doesn't fall far from the tree," to indicate that their daughters take after their mothers, then the wrinkles on their shrunken faces disappear. A spring of exaltation, of felicity, wells up in their refreshed hearts, they are suffused with pleasure and their maternal limbs are filled with a soothing balm.

Their daughters, amongst themselves, have many secrets, too; they know everything important that happens in their neighborhood, but they talk about these things more with their eyes than with their lips, because they take place quietly, confidentially and in secret.

And had the present disaster not spread its long, bony fingers savagely over the Pidvorki, were the disgrace not so abysmal and distressing, so dreadful and relentless, it, too, might have passed quietly. But since it is an unwonted, unspeakable tragedy—in all their history of young men and young women, brides and bridegrooms, such a thing had never happened here—it was therefore inevitable that sooner or later it would surface, that people would find out about it. Not the husbands, thank God for that; they know about nothing; they *dare not* know about anything. Only the Pidvorki wives know. But how long can you keep a thing like that concealed?

From early morning, things are already boiling and steaming among the women like a cauldron. They are not quarreling over their customers now, however; that is not even on their minds. This misfortune has struck them so hard that they have forgotten all about their own troubles.

Pressed tightly together like herring in a barrel, they are standing in a crowd, heatedly talking and arguing. Yet the passersby do not stop and listen. They see only that the women are sad, grave, downcast, ashamed to look at each other, as though they themselves had brought about this appalling state of affairs. A grievous blight, a shameful, yellow-black stain has appeared on everyone's head. An abomination has defiled their sanctity. And now like drowning persons, they are thrashing around for a way to save themselves.

They want to hide it, to prevent anyone from ever discovering it. They stand and think and wrinkle their already furrowed brows. All sorts of ideas whirl around in their heads, but no one has yet found the answer. No one has discovered a way by which they can ever disentangle themselves from the terrible net in which this evil thing has entrapped them.

Had a stranger chanced upon them at that moment, someone who did not know them but only heard of them, he, too, would have been shocked. Everything is different about the Pidvorki women now. Even the sun overhead, as though in embarrassment, is shooting out pale, meager, gold-tinged strips of light which lie like a burden upon the hearts of the women. The small gray-green clouds with their ragged edges, like foam-covered waves after a mild storm, are rushing about aimlessly; as they peer down at the crowd, they seem to be exchanging their own whispered confidences. Even the old willow tree, undoubtedly no stranger to such intricate secrets, also stands there dismayed. Its branches shake sorrowfully, dispiritedly, and the young green leaves look fearfully at each other, huddling close together as if they were afraid of the one mud-framed nest hidden among the shadowy, slender twigs at the treetop. But the nest itself is no happier than they. With a cold, guilty look it peeps out from behind the leaves, gazing wistfully into the distance. Even more dejected, more anxious, are the swallows hidden in the nest, as if they knew that

God was punishing the Pidvorki birds for their unpardonable sins because once, a long, long time ago, it was they who had carried the fire in their little beaks to destroy the Holy Temple in Jerusalem. God waits patiently, but He repays a hundredfold.

The peasants, driving slowly in their rickety carts, with no one stopping them, no one rushing forward to meet them, no one pulling at their sleeves and haggling with them, are surprised and disappointed. Have all the Jews fled?

But the Pidvorki women, caught up in this predicament, have completely forgotten that it is a market day. Arms folded, they stand around disconsolately, and to each one who joins them they turn with the anxious question:

"What shall we do? What shall we do?"

But no one has the answer. They cannot speak because they do not know what to say. Each one feels that a mass of molten wrath has poured down upon them from heaven, that an evil spirit had invaded their lives, and with every passing moment they are overtaken by new terrors. If they now do nothing, if they do not put an end to this nightmare, then God only knows what catastrophe might strike them next. None of them can be certain that tomorrow or the day after, the same lightning bolt will not seek out another one of them.

A sudden movement in the crowd. They grow so quiet they seem to be listening for a feeble voice to come out of the stillness itself. Their eyes widen, their lips twist in resentment and humiliation, their hearts beat more rapidly. Their tear-filled eyes look around to see what is happening.

With anger verging on fury a woman, waving her arms wildly, her eyes flashing and her voice trembling, summons them to action.

"Come with me, sisters! You'll see what I'm going to do! First I'll slap his face hard and then I'll thrash her! We must do whatever is necessary, so that nothing is left of them, not even a memory! We have no other choice!"

These pitiless words come from a tall, gaunt woman with broad shoulders, a woman who has earned the appellation of "Cossak" because with her own fists she drove off three burly peasants who had been trying to kill her husband for cheating them on weight—it was the first time he had ever helped her on a market day. . . .

"Don't scream so loud, Breindl!" someone begs.

"And why shouldn't I scream? You want me to hold my tongue about this? No, this is one thing I'm not going to swallow! I'll show those sinners they can't ruin the whole town!"

"But don't scream like that, Breindl!"

Breindele Cossak pays no attention. She clenches her right hand into a fist, waves it in the air and yells louder than ever.

"What's wrong with you, sisters? Why are you so scared? Look at you—quaking in your boots! That's the reason for all our troubles! Let's not act so scared today, then we won't have to hear tomorrow that our own daughters—they shouldn't live to see it, dear God!—are in the same kind of trouble!"

The women shuddered as if they had suddenly been doused with cold water. A few found the courage to support Breindl's proposal.

Sarah Leah said: "I agree! We should go! But only to him, to the bridegroom, and we should warn him—we will not let him make our town a laughing stock, and he must not humiliate her parents. The marriage must take place at once—today or tomorrow—before anybody finds out about it, and without any fuss—"

"No!" came an angry voice. "He doesn't deserve it—that we should come begging him for favors!"

Again they seemed to be at an impasse, but then a young voice rang out which made them all turn around to see who the speaker was. At first her voice shook, but then it grew firmer and firmer, each word clear and distinct.

"You are only fooling yourselves with that kind of nonsense! Who gave us the right to punish anyone, to hit people? And why torment her parents? Aren't they being punished enough already? If we really want to do something, the best plan is to say nothing about this to anyone, to keep calm, not to ask anybody's help, but to dig into our own pockets. Don't worry, God will return it to us. Let us now choose one or two of us to bring him the money quietly, so no one will know, because if we so much as whisper it, every child in town will soon be repeating it. We all know that walls have ears and streets have big eyes. . . ."

A great sigh of relief went up from all the women. Gratefully they looked at young Malkele—married only two months and already speaks so wisely. Her moderating words somehow eased the pressure of consternation and despair that threatened to overwhelm them. How much better she had made them feel! Each one regretted that the idea had not occurred to her first, but then, after all, Malkele was one of their own, a young wife of the Pidvorki. And it was all the more remarkable because they had not expected her—as a young girl she had already been known for her quick mind—to get involved with their troubles.

So now they began working on a plan to raise the money; it had to be done so as not to cause the slightest shadow of suspicion. Very quickly, however, it became evident that none of them could afford to give such large sums. Even if they all contributed beyond their means, the total would be nowhere what they needed. Amongst all of them they could raise two hundred, perhaps three, but the dowry was six hundred rubles, and now he had threatened to tear up the betrothal contract if they didn't give him a thousand! What would they do to him, he had taunted, take him to court?

Again panic overtook them. They stared at each other— perhaps someone had such a large sum hidden away? Each of them had her own "cache," but even if they put them all together it would have amounted to less than half the necessary sum.

Again a tumult of confused talk. Some of the women began hurling fire and brimstone at their own husbands, those lazy good-for-nothings who sat around idle all day. It had long been evident that their wives had no reason to be afraid of them, since they didn't lift a finger to earn their keep. For the same reason, it was also accepted that if the women sometimes needed money for a good cause, nobody had any right to question them about the why's and the wherefore's.

Some of the women still argued, however, that no matter what one thought of the men, they were older, and that it would therefore be no more than right to ask their advice.

Why should the women assume they knew better than the whole world? Other objected: just because one young woman had foolishly gotten herself into trouble, was that any reason for them to divorce their own husbands?

The voices grew louder, the shouting thunderous. Words flew like hail. No one listened to what the other was saying. They knew only one way to resolve the dilemma: yell, scream, curse. And they might have gone on this way all night had not Breindele Cossak, with her ear-splitting voice, begun to make a few of her words audible:

"*Me and Malkele have a plan—if you will only keep quiet and listen!*"

Suddenly the noise ceased, and the silence was as total as during the reading of the Eighteen Silent Benedictions. All eyes turned questioningly toward Malkele and Breindl, both of whom felt the blood rush to their faces. While Malkele had been speaking her golden words, Breindl had not left her side. Now she took a step forward and her shrill voice filled the vacuum of silence.

"Me and Malke have a plan. We'll all go and talk to Cha-vele, the doctor's wife. She is a smart and well-educated woman. We'll tell her the whole story from beginning to end and ask for her advice. If you feel too shy to talk to her, then leave it to me and Malke. But you all must come along with us. There's nothing to worry about. She's a good-hearted person and she'll listen. . . ."

A wan little smile settled like diamond dust on the lips of all the women. Their eyes brightened and they threw back their shoulders as though they were throwing off a heavy burden. Chavele was a kind, good woman; she was certain to give them sound advice. She was always doing things for them even before they asked her. It was she who had opened the school and who taught their children without taking a penny for it. Very often she accompanied her husband on his visits to poor sick patients and usually she left them a few coins for food. People said she had even written to the papers about the lives of the Pidvorki women, how hardworking and upstand-ing they were. . . . She loved them all very much; treated them as though they were her equal. And she knew about their lives because she was really interested, always asking them questions as if she were an ordinary housewife like they.

Yet they did live in two different worlds. They preferred that she not know too much about them. Somehow they wanted to find favor in her eyes, as if she—forgive the comparison—were a Christian woman. They themselves could not explain why they felt this way, but that's how it was.

They were extremely proud of the doctor's wife. They considered it an exceptional honor for them to have in their midst a cultured person like Chava, whom even the local squires respected, and therefore they now all smiled shyly whenever her name was mentioned. Almost in one voice they exclaimed: "Of course! Of course! Chavele will tell us what to do!" But all the time they were careful to keep their glances from meeting.

Malke understood these feelings and tried to reassure them. "Don't worry, it doesn't matter if she knows. She is a Jewish daughter, too, just like us. She won't tell a soul about it if we ask her not to. Such things happen—may they never happen, dear God!—even among the well-to-do. . . ."

After she spoke they all took a deep breath and started toward Chava's house on the hill. Like a column of soldiers they marched, shoulder to shoulder, heads high, faces shining with happiness and satisfaction.

Passersby, staring, stood aside to make way for them, tryint to guess what this extraordinary sight could possibly signify. Even their own husbands, puzzled, did not dare to go up to the women and ask where they were going.

With every step they grew more and more inspired by their mission. A firm determination, a deep sense of serving humanity drove them on. They were marching for a noble cause, they were crusading to prevent similar misfortunes from happening to others.

On their way to Chava's house they had first to traverse the entire length of the marketplace and its line of stalls that stood so close together they seemed to be holding hands. Then through a few narrow streets of peasant cottages with their thatched rooftops and tiny, timid-looking windows. Small as the cottages were, each one boasted a pair of acacia trees, whose white blossoms sent forth a fragrance that refreshed the entire neighborhood.

As the marchers emerged from these streets they were greeted by a lovely, flower-studded hill. At the left of this hill flowed a clear, quiet little stream which deceived even experienced travelers, so uncannily did it mirror the colors that grew on its banks. You had to come close to make sure that what your eyes saw was only an illusion. And the stream returned your stare with a kind of blank look that seemed to mock your puzzlement.

On top of the hill, adorned like a bride in garlands of blossoms, stood Chava's house, looking down pleasantly with its two large glass lamps under white shades, held in the right hands of two gleaming marble figures.

The long trek did not tire the women out. They strode briskly along, entertaining each other with biographical episodes similar to the one that had sent them on their present mission.

"You know," began Shifra the wholesaler, "mine tried the same trick on me, except I wasn't in that condition before the wedding, heaven forbid. He merely insisted that if we didn't give him another fifty rubles and a silver snuffbox—as we had promised him—he wouldn't go to the wedding canopy with me."

"A great misfortune that would have been!" someone laughed ironically.

"Yes," quipped a second. "If not Boruch, then it would have been Zoruch!"

The laughter that followed was halfhearted and polite, because not one of them really wished to leave her husband, despite the quarreling and the indignities. No matter how humiliating the insult, it was not as hurtful as being rejected, because after all, they still remained husband and wife— they quarreled and they made up, they made up and they quarreled.

When Chavele's house finally came into view they all cried out in one voice: "There it is!" and once more they forgot about themselves. Again they were zealots for a cause, again they became painfully aware that if they did not do everything possible now, the guilt would lie on their conscience like a rock.

As she considered what to say to Chavele, Malke's heart pounded more loudly than anyone else's. Good words, precise words, kept coming to mind, but she knew she would be unable to get them past her lips when she stood before Chava. If the other women were not there now, she would be more at ease.

She put it out of her mind. Whatever happened, would happen. Her heart, however, still refused to obey her; with every step she took it beat more wildly, and the sighs that tore out of her soul she tried to disguise as yawns, lest she alarm the other women.

Suddenly a voice exclaimed: "We're here! We're here!"

The women looked up, their eyes gladdened by the sight of beautiful, long-stemmed flowers arranged on a large, round table in the shade of a spreading willow. In the center of the table shone a silver samovar. In the still empty glasses played tiny rays of the setting sun as it sank rapidly behind the darkening blue hill.

"What welcome guests!" Chava greeted them with a gentle smile. Warm drops of kindliness and affection fell from her eyes upon their anxious hearts.

No expression of her face, no attitude of her body, showed the least surprise, as though she had eagerly been awaiting their arrival.

The women realized that Chavele was behaving with superb tact, and felt enormous guilt for disturbing her this way. But she merely excused herself to her other guests and invited the large group of women into her spacious summer parlor, for she had evidently surmised that what they had come to tell her was for her ears only.

But it did not go as they had planned. Breindele Cossak and the clever Malke, their two chosen representatives, now found it impossible to open their mouths. Chavele tried to help them out of their quandary.

"I'm sure it must be a matter of great importance that has brought you here," she smiled, "for otherwise I never get to see any of you."

But her pleasant words now made it more difficult than ever to tell this angelic woman their bad tidings. Each of them prayed in her heart that her own children might turn out even one-tenth as fine as Chava. They felt like putting their arms around her, kissing her, crying on her shoulder—and if she were moved to cry with them, it would be so much the sweeter.

Chavele, however, said not a word more. With her wide-open blue eyes which now filled up with compassion as she looked at her sisters, she tried to extract the pain and the awesome secret they had come to share with her. But her gentleness, her affable, encouraging look, only made them more hesitant, sealed their lips more tightly. The silence was now almost palpable. Barely breathing, they looked at each other through half-closed eyelids, trying to embolden each other, but mainly the two who had offered to speak for them. . . .

After a while, Chavele tried again, her voice sad but sweet. "Well, my dear sisters, can you not tell me a little of whatever it is that has brought you all here? If there is something I can do, I shall be most happy to do it. . . ."

Her glowing words were like balm upon their wounded hearts. "Dear sisters" she had called them! They—whose husbands never called them by any other name than "busy-bodies" and whose sons referred to them as *"yentes."*

To be sure, her language was not theirs. But God in heaven!—they felt nothing but goodness, tenderness, nobility in her "gentile" words. It was impossible *not* to feel it. Such courageous words from one of their own sisters, from a woman who belonged to their own people, who worshipped the same God—yes, she was one of their own! She was not so pious? How could God be displeased with such a generous, unselfish, hospitable creature? They themselves were prepared to accept punishment for her sins, if God so willed it—with the greatest of pleasure they would accept it. . . .

The sun had long set, leaving in its wake a blood-red streak which stared angrily at the women through the windows. The sky had grown somber and mysterious, the room darker. When Chavele began turning on lights, many of the women surreptitiously wiped their eyes. Realizing how difficult it was for them to speak, Chavele invited them to eat something, to have a glass of tea. But no one moved.

At last Malkele summoned up the courage to begin:

"Thank you, dear Chavele, but we are not hungry. . . . We did not come here to eat. We need your advice on a matter of great seriousness. . . .

A beginning having been made, Breindele was able to continue. Though she tried desperately to keep her voice low and soft, it emerged with its customary piercing quality.

"Our first request, Chavele, is that you speak with us in Yiddish. We are all, praise God, daughters of Israel—may our enemies roast in hell!"

Chava, who had been slowly nodding her head in agreement, blinked once and said almost inaudibly, "I will be happy to speak with you in whatever language you wish. Please go on."

"The story is this, Chavele. As you can see, we are ashamed to tell it to you, but since the lightning has struck, we must talk about it. We have no other choice. Esther Leah's Rochel—you know her? Eight weeks from today she is supposed to stand under the *chupah*. But we have learned that she—that that sinful woman is with child. And he, that cold-hearted scoundrel, now says that unless we add another five hundred rubles to her dowry, he won't marry her!"

Breindl's words affected Chavele visibly. She fully comprehended what a disaster this must be for them and regretted her own inadequacy to comfort them.

"I feel with you in your pain," she began softly. "But you must not despair. It is not a good situation, certainly, but such things do happen, unfortunately—" She was not sure how to continue.

"But what shall we do now, daughter?" came several voices at once. "That's why we have come here—so you can tell us what we must do!"

"Yes, Chavele—shall we give him the money—which we don't even have—or shall we tie a big rock around our own necks and jump into the river for shame?"

Now Chavele understood. It was not they who were now

speaking and imploring, but their terrible dilemma, their real fear of shame and disgrace. With deep sympathy she replied:

"What shall I say to you, dear sisters? You are the last ones in the world whom this tragedy should have struck— you who have so many difficult problems of your own. But since this dreadful thing has happened in our midst, we must be strong and not despair. We must think clearly and decide what is the wisest course to follow. In my opinion, the best thing we can do now is to help her get married as soon as possible. But even more important, we should try to prevent such things from ever happening in the future. It is not the first time, but it must be the last! Exactly what to do, how to do it, that I cannot tell you, because I don't know. However, if you need any help from me, you know I shall give it to you with all my heart. . . ."

Yes, now they knew. . . .

In an exalted mood they took leave of Chava and started homeward with a clear sense of what still remained to be done, but certain that this would prevent further tragedy and disgrace. They could have shouted for joy, embraced the hill, the river, the peasant cottages and each other.

The knowledge that Chavele was with them in their struggle had renewed their courage. Now the whole town would be on their side. Covered by the dusk, they marched back to the Pidvorki, strong, bold, reassured. The massive blank wall obstructing their decision began to recede. Listening to their humming and buzzing, one sensed that they were being led by some fiery spirit and that the further along their course they proceeded, the farther away they would drive this evil thing, this ugliness that had struck at them.

Their stride became more vigorous, more determined; their eyes shone more brightly, their hearts grew fuller, their buzzing and humming louder, stormier. The air itself trembled as the piercing tones penetrated deeper and deeper into their souls. The crowd of women grew quiet as they listened to this resolute voice of victory:

"I tell you, sisters: We must not touch them, neither one

of them! But this coming Shabbos we must all gather as one person, and we must burst into the synagogue during the Torah reading. And we shall not let the men continue the reading until they promise to accept our plan of excommunication—yes, *excommunication*!"

"Breindl is right!"

"No! We must tear him to pieces!"

"We must dress him in *tallis* and *kittel* and he must stand amidst the burning black candles and swear—"

"Yes! Yes! He must swear!"

Again the noise grew louder, more intense. They did not let one another finish speaking. Like sharp, poisonous arrows their words collided in midair and fell to the ground. In each of the women burned the identical hellfire of hate and anger, revenge and the enforcement of justice. Each new opinion was immediately and noisily supported amidst a gnashing of teeth and a bellicose clenching of fists. . . .

Nature herself became alarmed by the scene. The clouds began racing to and fro across the sky, the stars changed places with each other, the wind whistled and the trees shook, the frogs croaked insistently, and all this fused together with the protests of the women, joined their unrestrained commotion, seething and boiling up into a deafening outcry, until one voice rose above the others.

"Sisters! Sisters! I have a proposal! Let us all go to the synagogue courtyard right now! Let's climb up on the mill-stones and shout aloud our decision so that everyone will know!"

"She's right! Yes! To the courtyard!" The assent came from a hundred other voices.

Bound together by the cord of triumph, arms linked, faces radiant, eyes blazing, they marched toward the synagogue. As they entered the streets of the town they fell on each other's necks and kissed each other joyfully, their eyes brimming over. Now there was not the slightest doubt in their minds: this was the best, the wisest, the most practical plan, and it would protect them from future shame and embitterment.

Fear filled the hearts of the Pidvorki inhabitants when they heard the loud tramping of the women's feet.

Young and old, men and women, followed them to the courtyard of the synagogue. With bloodless faces the towns-folk watched to see what unprecedented event they were about to witness. The eyes of the young men darted uneasily around the crowd; the young women hid their faces in each other's shoulders and inwardly wept. . . .

Agile as a cat, Breindele Cossak clambered up on the highest millstone. Her very first words struck the ears of the crowd like cannon-shot.

"An awful thing, a shameful thing, has happened in our midst! We cannot keep it hidden any longer! We don't want to keep it hidden! Therefore, the women of this town have decided to place under excommunication—"

The clamor was so loud, so fierce, so explosive, that her next words were not heard. But in an instant, everyone there knew whose name she had uttered.

When the uproar had subsided, Breindl continued:

"One more thing! We demand that neither he, nor any of his family or friends should be allowed to approach the Torah! We demand that until the marriage ceremony is over, no one shall have any dealings with them whatsoever!"

"Right! Right!" came an echoing thunder.

"No one must lend them anything, no one must borrow anything from them, no one must even come within four feet of them! And as for her—we will lock her up until the child is born. No one will see her! And when her time comes, we will take her to the graveyard and there in the farthest corner she will give birth to her child."

"That's what she deserves!"

"The wedding will take place during the day—and with-out any music!"

"Right! And let this be a lesson!"

When Breindl finished, others climbed up on the stones and shouted their agreement or offered further suggestions for punishing the guilty pair.

"On the day of the wedding," one proposed, "black can-dles must be lit all over the Pidvorki, and during the seating ceremony of the bride and groom, all the girls must encircle the bride, and the *badchan* must recite a warning that this is what shall be done to any Jewish daughter who does not keep herself pure, as prescribed by our Torah, and thereby brings disgrace to the whole community—"

"Yes! Yes!"

"That's how it should be!"

"Apostates!"

Like chunks of heavy, jagged metal these last words split the hearts of the listeners. A deadly pallor, the reflection of an unfamiliar terror, covered every face. In the boiling cauldron of shame and anguish their feelings seethed and simmered. What had they done? What had happened to the tranquil life they had led before this disaster? Exhausted, demeaned, their hearts hammering, the pupils of their eyes darker and more frightened, they broke the silence with a glimmer of hope that barely illuminated their gloom, and very very slowly the crowd began to disperse. . . .

Doctor Machover

I   In a small south-Russian town which curls helplessly about itself on the right bank of the Dnieper River, Moyshe-Dovid Machover was born to well-to-do, earnestly devout parents. His mother and father were content: they served God sincerely and He had prospered them.

Along this same path they were determined to lead their one and only child, their pride and joy, their most precious possession.

On his sixth birthday, Moyshe-Dovid's father wrapped him in a big *tallis* and carried him in his arms to the *Bes-Medresh*. Inside the house of worship he strode purposefully to the Ark of the Torah and sat the boy down on the bottom step. With heartfelt reverence he took the hem of the holy curtain in his hand and very carefully touched it to each of the boy's eyes. Then, after pressing the curtain to his own lips, he spoke these chilling words to God:

"*Riboynoy-shel-oylom*! Master of the Universe! This child, this blood of my blood and flesh of my flesh, I now bring to Thee. This son of mine, with whom Thou hast blessed me, I offer to Thee that he may walk uprightly in Thy paths, that he may study Thy Torah, that he may serve Thee and only

Thee. And rather than he should choose *not* to walk in Thy ways, it were far better that he be unable to walk at all! And rather than he should ever choose to abandon Thy holy Torah, it were better that the spirit of life abandon his body! And rather than he should choose to desert Thy house for other gods, it were better that he be unable to move at all, but that they carry him out—hear me, O Lord of the Universe—it were better that they carry him out in his shroud!"

The child's head snapped up in shocked surprise as he stared wide-eyed and incredulous at his father. When their eyes met, the older Machover shouted at the top of his voice:

"Moyshe-Dovid! Listen to me! You *must* grow up to be a righteous man!"

The child, as well as all the other worshippers in the synagogue—the building itself, it seemed—quaked under this uncompromising command.

From that time forward, Moyshe-Dovid could be found in the *Bes-Medresh* every day of the week. Early in the morning he went there with his teacher. Walking a little distance behind them was his mother, shedding copious tears of joy. In the evening, when Moyshe-Dovid returned home after a long day's studying, his father would also read with him for a little while. And thus it went until the boy knew more than anyone in the town could teach him. Thereafter he began studying the sacred texts on his own.

The wheel of life rolled on in its customary cycle. Years came and went. Time, that most illusive of all mysteries, passed imperceptibly, like the last fading notes of a musical chord vanishing into the air.

2   Illimitable was the happiness of Moyshe-Dovid's parents when they realized that good fortune was leading them by the right hand. How beneficent was their God! No sooner had He heard their prayers and accepted their laudations when He blessed them with a child, a son with all the virtues: sound in health, pleasing in appearance, and most important of all—the gift of genius. Truly, a prize for God, an ornament for his parents, and a blessing for his people.

"*Riboynoy-shel-oylom*! We thank Thee when we lie down and we thank Thee when we rise up!" With this ancient prayer Moyshe-Dovid's parents tried to express the boundless gratitude that was in their hearts for the blessings God had bestowed upon them.

Only once—when Moyshe-Dovid was ten years old—did he cause them a bit of heartache. But it soon passed and their only son regained his customary composure. They saw this as a sign from heaven. God, blessed be His name, had merely been testing them, and He had not prolonged the trial. It happened this way:

One night, awakened from sleep, Moyshe-Dovid's mother heard her son apparently speaking to someone in his room. She sat up, leaned over the bed, and noticing that there was no light coming from the room, she grew alarmed. She woke her husband and they both tiptoed over to Moyshe-Dovid's door. Listening closely, they were terrified. In his sleep, their son was reciting long passages from the Prophets! They were afraid to awaken him, but neither could they go back to sleep. Until daybreak they sat and listened.

The Prophets! Unbeknownst to anyone, including his teacher, the boy had been studying the Prophets! And already knew whole sections by heart! So it was also possible, God forbid, that he was looking into other forbidden writings, words that could lead him away—ineffable thought!—from the path of righteousness.

They could hardly wait for Moyshe-Dovid to awaken. They took him into their room, locked the door against prying ears, and demanded that he confess. Unaware that he was guilty of any wrongdoing, Moyshe-Dovid, without fear or hesitation, admitted to reading other books of the Bible in addition to the Five Books of Moses.

Disturbed and perplexed, they pleaded with him to stop studying the Prophets until he was at least sixteen. As a reward, they promised him the most expensive gifts, but the boy could not understand what they wanted of him. Why were his father and mother so insistent that he stop studying the Prophets when he enjoyed those writings so much? And since nothing his parents said could convince him, he continued reading the inspired words of Isaiah, Amos, Micah, Jeremiah. . . .

His parents now began checking on every move he made, suspecting a hidden motive for his interest in the Prophets—and who knows what other forbidden texts he might be reading. But they were only deluding themselves. Moyshe-Dovid was concealing nothing. In the *Bes-Medresh* and at home he pursued his studies openly. The few halfhearted slaps that his father administered had no effect whatsoever.

Whenever Moyshe-Dovid found himself alone in the synagogue or at home, he would lock the door, place a few chairs around a table, and in the role of an old Hebrew Prophet, castigate the Jews for their sins. His eyes glowing, his face flaming and perspired, he would declaim entire chapters of Amos and Isaiah until his voice cracked.

For months he lived with this sweet, innocent hope, full of faith and certitude that when he grew up he would be a prophet to the Children of Israel. Once, he even suggested to his parents that they take him to the graves of those ancient visionaries. He insisted on questioning them about the Prophets, about God, about Jewish history. They could not answer him, and his questions filled them with dread.

"My child is lost to me, lost . . .," Moyshe-Dovid's father lamented, and whenever this terrifying thought recurred to him, he wept bitterly. He took vows upon himself to do philanthropic deeds, if only God would show His mercy and return Moyshe-Dovid to him. He gave liberally to charitable causes and performed other praiseworthy services for the community.

And God did not fail him. Soon the boy's parents noticed a change for the better in his behavior, although in truth, the prophetic spirit, which his childish understanding could not really grasp, bubbled within him until the time of his bar mitzvah.

In his thirteenth year he began to comprehend the Talmud in greater depth. He had already read through many Jewish books on ethics and morals which his father called to his attention in the hope they might inspire him to become a writer, a consummation that would have fulfilled the fondest dreams of his parents. And as it turned out, the desire to write did take root in Moyshe-Dovid's mind. He began studying even more zealously, immersing himself completely in his talmudic studies.

3 In this way, Moyshe-Dovid spent seventeen long, arduous years between the high, drab and silent walls of the *Bes-Medresh*. From the age of six to twenty-three, in the grip of an overpowering urge to know and to understand, he swam in the depths of the talmudic seas. For Moyshe-Dovid the Talmud was a fresh, inexhaustible spring. The more he drank from it, soaking the waters up like a sponge, the more there remained for him to drink. He became as familiar with all the traditional Jewish texts and their commentaries as a daring swimmer is with his hometown river.

Soon the entire Orthodox Jewish world came to look upon Moyshe-Dovid as a unique blessing; they put all their hopes in him, as if he were destined to be the Messiah, the Great Redeemer, the brilliant star whose light would dispel the gloom and darkness of Exile.

Moyshe-Dovid wrote several religious books in which he gave voice to all the despair and hopelessness of the diaspora Jew. With each passing day he himself became more devout, more firm in his belief. People began referring to him affectionately as Moyshe-Dovidl, as if he were a sage or a Hasidic rabbi, and as they pronounced his name, their hearts beat more rapidly and the blood coursed more swiftly in their veins.

From all over the Jewish world, people began coming to Moyshe-Dovid for his blessing, but his spirit was too noble to permit him to be drawn into that sort of adulation. Moyshe-Dovid believed in God with that unshakable faith that dries up oceans, extinguishes suns and stops the rotation of the earth, for he who truly believes in the goodness of the Almighty puts no trust in human miracles.

4 In the twenty-third year of his life something extraordinary happened to Moyshe-Dovid which neither his parents nor his friends—nor even he himself—could have anticipated.

Without knowing where it came from—or why—he sensed that a truth, a terrible truth, was struggling to become clear to him. Before his thirsty eyes, which had eagerly swallowed so much of Jewish learning, a kind of pale light was fluttering weakly and indeterminately; it did not emanate from an original source but was reflected indirectly from somewhere else. It happened after Moyshe-Dovid, having come upon an old book of ethics, was leafing through its yellowed pages. He had almost finished with it and was about to replace it on the shelf when his eye fell on a fading inscription on the inside back cover. As he read it again, more carefully, beads of perspiration formed on his forehead. He could not believe his eyes.

"Dear Reader," the message began in a neat, firm, Hebrew script. "Whether you are young or old, scholar or uneducated, no matter who or what you may be, you are nonetheless my brother. So you are close and important to me, especially since this book is now in your hands. I ask you to read carefully what I have written here and to think about it most seriously. Do not take my word for it; seek the truth for yourself until you find it. And if you agree with me, then teach it to a good friend. But know once and for all that everything printed in this book—and many others like it—is falsehood and lies. There is *no* God, there is *no* Hell, there is *no* Paradise. It is all falsehood and lies!"

Moyshe-Dovid did not believe a word of this inscription, but something drove him to read it again and again. Everything about it was puzzling. For one thing, who was the author of these incredible words? For another, how could he have the insolence to write such blasphemies in a holy book? If only he could find out whose words these were—Moyshe-Dovid thought to himself as his right hand clenched into a tight fist—he would soon settle accounts with that apostate!

In no way could he make peace with those sacrilegious sentences, yet something compelled him to read them over and over again. And each time he read them he grew more incensed. He paced back and forth across the *Bes-Medresh*. He picked up the book again. He would rip off the whole cover and grind it into the dust, along with those heretical words that brazenly mocked the name of God, blessed be He.

As he read the few Hebrew sentences once more, an idea came to him. Why not let the book just lie there openly on the table and watch to see who picks it up? Perhaps that would give him a clue. The thought cooled his anger somewhat and enabled him to think more clearly. No, his plan was too risky. No good would come of it, anyway. Perhaps it would be better just to keep his eyes and ears open. He put the offending volume inside his own lectern. Whenever he was alone in the *Bes-Medresh* he reread the inscription and thought about it.

It still seemed to him that he had only to learn a little bit more and everything would become clear to him. What that "little bit more" was, however, continued to elude him. Furthermore, a whole series of weighty questions now arose in his mind. New worlds were being revealed to him—and there was no one he could talk with about them. And even if he could find someone to listen, what would he say?

Where were all these questions coming from? And why did one question always lead to another? Moyshe-Dovid was appalled by his own thoughts. It is forbidden even to ask such questions! Whoever asks them is already half a heretic. But he was still a true believer, was he not?

He did not know where to look for the answers. He felt like a person suddenly awakened in a dark room. Was it night? Day? God only knows. God? Ha!

5 For Moyshe-Dovid each day was a long, difficult year. But the nights—at night he was free of the whole external world. The nights belonged to him alone, and he would spend them engrossed in his quest for truth. Each night was an eternity during which his soul kept sinking deeper into an abyss of doubt. Yet something impelled him to continue his search for the source of the ray of light that had appeared to him. That was his quest.

One day when he was alone in the *Bes-Medresh* it occurred to him to look through all the volumes in the bookcases; perhaps he would find the kind of book he needed, the very one he was searching for. Leaving his Talmud folio open on the lectern, he went from one bookcase to the next, opening each volume and leafing through it. Perhaps this would be the one. Perhaps that one. But he found nothing.

As he shut the last bookcase and turned to go back to his seat near the Holy Ark, he paled in fright. All the lecterns, the tables and benches, the posts of the reading platform—they had linked arms and were blocking his way back, as if to say:

"Well, Moyshe-Dovid, now are you satisfied?"

He turned and ran to the door. What kind of tricks was his imagination playing on him?

When he finally grew a little calmer it was quite late in the afternoon. He felt ashamed of himself, of his weakness. For hours he wandered aimlessly through the back streets of the town. By the time he returned to the synagogue the evening prayers had already been said. The whole congregation stared at him in amazement as he entered and took his seat. It was the first time in his life he had ever missed a service, but it never even occurred to anyone that Moyshe-Dovid, their pride and their treasure, had not said the afternoon and evening prayers wherever he had been. That was simply unthinkable!

And that they did not even suspect him, that their faith in him was still solid as a rock, was in itself a source of extreme disquietude to him.

Moyshe-Dovid continued his daily attendance at the **6** *Bes-Medresh*, but he found it more and more difficult to concentrate on his studies. He kept turning over in his mind the ideas that had arisen to plague him. And when the possibility occurred to him that he might have to leave the *Bes-Medresh*, where he had spent so many years—where his imagination had been developed and sharpened, where he had dreamed the great dream of one day being useful to his people, of leading it in God's ways, he burst into prolonged weeping.

And weeping with him were the Holy Ark, the Torah scrolls, the bimah, the old rickety lecterns, the broken tables and benches, the gray brick walls, the roof, the floor, the entire building.

His big eyes, in which doubt contended with faith, were filled with fear as he approached the Holy Ark. With trembling hands he parted the curtains, opened both doors, and putting his head inside the Ark, he called out:

"Master of the Universe! For twenty-three years you have led me on the path of righteousness. Do not forsake me now. I shall be devoted to you body and soul, but have mercy upon me—do not deprive me of my faith. Cease your testing of me. Help me to overcome temptation. *Riboynoy-shel-oylom!* Do not destroy my faith in you!"

His voice resounded in every corner of the synagogue with terror and dismay.

When Moyshe-Dovid withdrew his head from the Ark he felt, for the first time and with a sense of shock, the shakiness of his former steadfast faith.

Was it so very long ago—before the worm of doubt had settled in his heart and begun gnawing away at his faith—that he had felt so serene, so much at peace with himself?

In deep sorrow, with the weight of this unsolved riddle on his weary shoulders, Moyshe-Dovid slowly and painstakingly, step by step, made his way home.

7   With the vigor that belongs only to young people thirsting for truth, Moyshe-Dovid devoured one book after another. Tirelessly he continued his search for the ray of light that had revealed itself to him. He understood that this light must emanate from a vast sun and that what was required of him now was to shunt aside all the obstacles—the accumulated towering mountains that obstructed the light, and only then would the full sun emerge in all its beauty and splendor.

What those sun-concealing mountains consisted of, Moyshe-Dovid had no idea, but he was certain that the more books he read—and now he was reading them with completely different eyes—the brighter that ray would grow, and the more distinct its outlines.

It was not a waste of time. Moyshe-Dovid realized full well that he was going astray; he knew it as certainly as one who is awakened by a disturbing dream in which he has seen the truth. Though he was no longer studying Talmud, he came to the *Bes-Medresh* every day as usual. With the single-minded determination of a child attempting to unravel a knot he continued to follow the thread as far as it would lead him. When he had unraveled almost half of it, he realized he was not proceeding in the desired direction. Providence had erred in giving the loose end of the knot into his hand. That he had not himself been looking for it was half a consolation. He would never have been able to forgive himself for this sin if he had picked it up of his own volition.

And when he realized that he was going in the wrong direction, he was even happier. Now he must not lose another minute in beginning his search for the other end of the knot.

The search, however, brought him only acute spiritual anguish. Every morning for a month he betook himself to a nearby forest, where he would stay until far into the night. Here he would go from one tree to the other, his arms folded across his chest, pondering the terrible truth that had been revealed to him. Often he would stop before the oldest tree in the forest—"the Centenarian," he named it—and for hours at a time, hardly aware of what he was doing, stand there peeling the bark and thinking.

At home and throughout the town, people began to notice his absence. Why should a young man vanish for days at a time? No one had the temerity, however, to mention it openly. Was Moyshe-Dovid going into the woods to concentrate on some particularly difficult section of the Talmud? Such things were not unheard of.

As for Moyshe-Dovid, he was becoming more and more keenly aware that his Jewish studies were inadequate for him and the *Bes-Medresh* too restricting. With the mute pain of a mother compelled to leave her babies in the hands of strang-

ers, Moyshe-Dovid Machover finally left his shtetl, his parents, and the *Bes-Medresh* and set out to see what he could
find in the big wide world.

        In the world outside, Moyshe-Dovid found content-
8 ment. And again he found it in study. There was so
        much to learn! He rushed from one book to another as
though he wanted to swallow the whole treasury of human
knowledge in one gulp. Without measure and without order
he read and he studied. He was the happiest of happy people—
he had discovered God. For fifteen years Moyshe-Dovid lived
exclusively in the world of ideas, avoiding any contact with
real life.

        And because he lived not in the present but in the future,
these fifteen years seemed to him like fifteen days. He did not
even notice that God, with His strong arm, was regularly
moving the hour hand of life round and round. And when
time began to demand an accounting from Moyshe-Dovid, he
listened very seriously to its enchanting speech. The language
of life is without tone and without sound, yet what heavenly
music it is! And this divine music painted heavenly pictures
for the eyes of Dr. Machover. In those images he recognized
his calling, the path he must follow, the work he must do.

        Insofar as his time was concerned, Dr. Machover soon
arrived at a reasonable arrangement: half he spent in doing
translations—which provided him with life's necessities—
and half he devoted to the study of science.

        He was now completing a work in which he convincingly
showed, with the force of all his accumulated knowledge, that
religion is a negative influence in society.

        The advancement of human knowledge became Dr.
Machover's supreme ideal. He believed in it with all the fire
of his soul and all the nobility of his spirit. It became his only
god. He regarded each branch of science as a single link in a
chain, and only by joining all the links together could Man
create the golden chain of human knowledge. It goes without
saying that each link must fit perfectly into the next; if one of
the links is faulty, the entire chain will fall apart. Moreover,

even if only one of the links is made of spurious gold, the entire chain is weakened and may collapse.

Dr. Machover was certain, however, that in his chain every link was made of real gold and that all the links had been fused together permanently by the powerful hand of human knowledge itself. He believed this in the same steadfast way that he had once believed in the Jewish God.

And being by nature an enthusiast, he hoped that his book would open the eyes of many people, that many of the blind would be enabled to see, that they would prefer to believe in human intelligence, experience and knowledge rather than in an unknowable God. More and more confidently he strode along the path that he himself had laid out with so much effort.

9 His book, *The Truth About God*, which the publisher had accepted and then suddenly rejected, was finally published by Dr. Machover himself. Far from being discouraged by this, he now planned a second book which he had been dreaming about even before he wrote the first one. In his second book Dr. Machover expounded his thesis that the Jewish people must be the first to give up its religion. Other peoples who renounce their god have their own country, their own culture, a deep-rooted literary tradition. They therefore need have no fear of losing their identity. The Jews, however, because they lack all that, must prepare themselves all the sooner for the time when they will have to live without a religion.

At this point the wheel of Dr. Machover's fortune slipped a gear, stopped altogether, and then began turning the other way.

A child, a lovable child whom Dr. Machover himself had nurtured, the son of his best friend and confidant, fell seriously ill. With the boy's kidneys not functioning, he was doomed to die in a very short time. The resultant upheaval in Dr. Machover's life was violent. Where was science? Why was his great god of Science suddenly so helpless? Was there still a heaven somewhere that concealed a God?

Leading specialists were called in. They prescribed the routine remedies, though none of the doctors really believed they would be effective in this case. When the hot baths failed to induce sweating, they recommended cupping. Nothing helped.

Dr. Machover lost all faith in their methods. But where had his brains been all this time? So long as he had not been confronted with this cold fact head-on, a fact known to him for many years, he had remained indifferent to it. Why? If science was helpless against one illness, who could guarantee that it would fare better in other instances? How many other links in the golden chain were made of mock gold? For if they can gild one link with such false glitter, they can also blind the eyes with others. Why were these counterfeit links included at all—was it out of self-interest or out of ignorance?

The true believer in science, in human intelligence and experience, was suddenly immobilized, impotent, did not know where to turn. The more he listened to the talk of the doctors, the more he saw of their methods, the worse grew his feeling of emptiness. With their cynical ignorance the doctors were sucking the faith out of his soul like leeches. Human helplessness had impinged upon his own personal life, but why should the doctors delude themselves and the whole world, too? Why were they convinced that they did know? Let them not be ashamed to admit their own blindness—it would result in less tragedy.

However, the ignorance of the doctors must not be the end of the story. Dr. Machover knew there were libraries containing the whole treasury of human knowledge and experience. He would go back to the source.

Like a drowning man clutching at straws, Dr. Machover reached for the findings of the foremost authorities in medical science. He searched, studied, researched. Nothing!

The science of medicine records dry facts: such and such happened; but it could also have happened otherwise. Why it happened, and why it could also be otherwise, to these questions they had no answers.

Dr. Machover began to feel as if he were walking on a

treadmill. The wheel turns more and more rapidly, and if you are not careful you can fall and break your neck. He began to feel that the ground—which he himself had plowed—was slipping away from under his feet, and he didn't want to fall. And under such circumstances, no one offers you any sympathy. People only laugh at you.

10 When Dr. Machover visited his friend the next day, and the next, and they had called in other doctors—all of them famous specialists in their field—and these men advised the same course of treatment as the previous physicians, Dr. Machover accused them in a voice that shook with emotion:

"Why don't you stop tormenting the child! You don't even have any faith yourselves in what you're doing!"

He went over to the boy, who had just been taken out of the bathtub. The child's cheeks were red as two beautiful apples, his black curly hair was tousled, his body white and fresh, but his eyes, which already held the presence of death, spoke silently, eloquently, to Dr. Machover.

"You grown-ups—you are so big, so healthy, so strong; you know so much; for thousands of years you have studied and studied—look at me, good people! Help me to live! Do it for the sake of my mother, who risked her life for me. Do it for the sake of my father, who weaves such hopeful dreams for me in the dim light of dawn. And do it for me—still a baby who has not yet had a chance to live, to see anything. I have so much faith in your knowledge. I have faith in my teacher, in my father, in my mother, in Dr. Machover. Look at me, have pity on me. . . ."

Dr. Machover's broad forehead paled. A streak of black dirt settled in the middle of it, a sign of mourning—his last world had been destroyed.

Lowering himself to the floor on his knees, he spoke softly to the child: "Forgive me, Sholem, I have sinned against you. We have all sinned against you—the whole world!"

Dr. Machover's friend rushed over and raised him from the ground. "What are you doing, Moyshe-Dovid!"

Taking the boy's head in his hands and kissing it, Dr. Machover said: "Shloymke, spit on me!"

"What on earth are you saying, Moyshe-Dovid!" his friend protested.

"I deserve it! I deserve it!"

Without another word to anyone, Dr. Machover left the house.

Four days later the child was dead.

Coming into his study, Dr. Machover thought to him-
11 self: "With one of my hands I can support twenty children, but in this case, with both hands, with my brain,
with my soul, together with all the leading medical authorities, we could not even help one small, unfortunate child. . . ."

He opened all his bookcases and sat down on the bare floor. As he looked around at the hundreds of volumes, tears rolled down his white cheeks and disappeared into his bushy black beard. His large, husky frame was convulsed by sobs.

It was only the second time in his life that the innermost recesses of his soul had wept. The first time had been twenty-five years ago, when he had mourned for his lost faith in the Jewish God.

Coldly, almost indifferently, Dr. Machover ripped up all his manuscripts, and with each tearing motion he kept repeating, "What is Man? What is God? What is faith?"

After a while he began answering his own questions. "Man is a creature who has a god. An individual who has no god cannot be counted among the humans. Without a god, without a faith, a person is like a destroyed ancient world, a heap of rubble baked by the sun and soaked by the rain, a world that someone may dig up one day and write a book about."

Was he himself not a book, a whole book, like those in his bookcases? Each book is a world, a thousand-year-old world that disappeared from the world arena a long long time ago, almost forgotten now by history. The difference between the books and himself is only that they existed in certain defined periods and he, Moyshe-Dovid Machover, lives with them in *all* periods.

He lost all track of time. He knew only that day followed night, night—the day. He gave up studying, even reading. He felt painfully the absence of faith. With his own intelligence he must discover what kind of being "Man" is, what kind of being "God" is, and wherein lies the difference between them. If he, Moyshe-Dovid Machover, is a creature called "Man," he should at least be able to understand himself.

12 Once more he began studying the behavior of his fellow human beings and what their faith consists of. He observed silently, without speaking, like a guest on his first visit.

One day a woman came into his office. She was old, sick, could barely stand. Before he could even ask her what she wanted, she was on the floor at his feet, sobbing:

"Doctor, Doctor, God and you must save my son!"

"You've come to the wrong place, my dear woman. I am not that kind of doctor."

"I beg you, Doctor! He is my breadwinner, my *kaddish*, the sole comfort in my lonely life!"

She could have moved a stone to tears.

"My dear woman, you must go to a medical doctor—"

"I will not go anywhere else, Doctor, even if I stay here till I die! You must come with me now—"

Dr. Machover's face turned chalk-white. He grew thoughtful, shook his head. His eyes flashed.

"Listen to me, my good woman. Go home now. Tell your son that the doctor said he is better, that he must get out of bed and go to his work as usual."

The woman's eyes opened wide in alarm. "Dr. Machover, what in heaven's name—for three weeks he has not even been able to turn over in bed without help. For the last four days he hasn't been able to eat or drink anything. The doctors have given up on him—"

"Go home! Make him swallow a spoonful of cold water.

Tell him what I just said. He will get well, I promise you!"

When the woman left, Dr. Machover laughed, a wild, mocking laughter. Wringing his hands, he paced back and forth across the room, shaking his head accusingly. He, Doctor Machover, had prescribed a spoonful of cold water for a man who was more dead than alive! Maybe the water would finish him off!

Why was he torturing himself this way?

Two days later the old woman was back. Again she was kneeling at his feet, but this time the tears in her eyes were tears of gratitude.

"God and you have saved my son, my sole provider—how can I thank you enough, Doctor?"

Dr. Machover could not conceal his astonishment and his fear.

During the next few days the woman could think of nothing else but this miracle that the good doctor Machover had performed for her sake. Wherever she went she told the story of the doctor who had saved her son's life after all the "big doctors" had given up. The news spread like an electric current through the Jewish quarter, and those who heard it, believed it.

From all corners, people made their way to Dr. Machover's door. His first response was to lock and bolt it.

Those who had come for help, however, refused to budge. For days at a time they stood outside his door, weeping. Their tears penetrated the walls of the house and found their way to the doctor's conscience.

"Doctor Machover! True, you lost your faith, your soul is aflame with anger. It is a terrible thing to live with, but why should you not help to extinguish that fire and ease your own suffering by wiping away the tears of other human beings? Do you know, Moyshe-Dovid, what it means to wipe away your brother's tears, to lighten a troubled soul? Do it, Moyshe-Dovid! It will not cause you any pain. You will not thereby deny your own soul. You can tell us what to do, just as you told that old woman. Laugh at yourself if you wish, drown in your own bitter laughter, but help us! Look at our faces, gaze deeply into our eyes—you will see all our sorrow and despair there. And by helping us, Moyshe-Dovid, perhaps you will help yourself. . . ."

Every day of the week, people came to Dr. Machover seeking his help, and every day those he had helped came back to thank him.

What could it all signify?

Did it not mean that human beings need faith as they need air to breath? It did not matter much what one believed in, so long as one believed in *something*—that was the significant part, and that was the discovery his own misfortune had led him to. Most likely, people have known this for a long time. But he had arrived at that conclusion by virtue of his own experience.

It was also clear now to Dr. Machover how Jesus Christ had become a god—he had *believed* he was a god. His faith was so powerful that it had forced the world to believe and to recognize him as a god. Judas Iscariot had been the most unfortunate man in the world because he was cursed with disbelief.

Dr. Machover now found himself longing for a faith of his own. Faith began calling to him enticingly. He was certain about that. He heard it as clearly as a midnight walker in the forest who suddenly hears his name called.

If he was to be a believer, then closest to his heart was the Jewish God, the God of Abraham, Isaac and Jacob.

At the moment he silently pronounced the names of the three patriarchs, Dr. Machover was suffused with a strange warmth. Even admitting that those ancestors may never have existed, admitting that they are only myths by which we designate certain historic epochs or worlds or even eternities, those names were nonetheless dear to him, they comforted his soul and exalted his spirit.

With a mingling of joy and pain Dr. Machover felt that he was again a believer—but now he was a believer in faith itself. To those who came to him for help he would offer this word of consolation: "God will help. Have faith!"

A rumor spread that Dr. Machover was again a devoutly

observant Jew who prayed three times a day. Every morning several people appeared outside his home to see for themselves. At six o'clock they were already gathering. The weaker-willed among them made no attempt to hide their curiosity or their feelings. They peered brazenly into windows, they argued about Dr. Machover's "conversion" at the top of their voices, so that not only the doctor heard what was going on but the whole neighborhood as well.

"With my own ears I heard him reciting the verse, 'I will betroth myself to Thee forever'!"

"Me, too! I also heard him!"

"No doubt about it—he's *davening*!"

The Jewish intellectuals of the town now avoided Dr. Machover whenever possible. If they had to pass his home they walked on the opposite side of the street and kept their heads down, as if they didn't want to see what was going on there.

Some of them felt, deep in their hearts, that Moyshe-Dovid Machover was not altogether wrong. Others felt that they themselves were somehow responsible—if not completely, then at least in part—for what had happened to him, although they couldn't have told you why or how.

Every evening, when Dr. Machover took his daily walk, many pairs of searching, inquisitive eyes followed him. People walking in the same path stepped aside. But Dr. Machover continued toward his destination without even looking around. His gait was slow and measured, in time to the clicking of his thick mahogany walking stick against the sidewalk. A calm and gentle aura, free of passion, hovered about him, like the falling of fresh white snow.

There had once been a time when people approached him with awe; now it was with fear. Once, people had immersed and sanctified themselves in his glance; now they see eyes that are cold and deep, the hidden source of secrets still untapped. . . .

The Mysterious Secret

I   AT FAR TOO tender an age she began to feel the oppressive weight of life's burdens. She was much too young to withstand the deadly arrows which, one after the other, penetrated her young, beautiful head and lacerated her wonderfully perceptive soul. When she was only fourteen the blood began to drip from her heart. At that time, when her spiritual world was still sparse, when she was not yet armored by any of life's scars, she was already bending like a young sapling whose trunk is not strong enough to resist the buffeting winds. Already her young mind was preoccupied with serious and knotty questions that were far beyond her powers.

For hours at a time she would walk about, lost in thought, arms folded across her chest, her face tense and somber, as she searched for the answer to one basic question: What was at the bottom of all the deception and the lying in her family— by her mother to her father, by her father to her mother, by her sister to her husband, by the children to the parents and by the parents to the children? Why, although they were of the same flesh and blood, were they nonetheless strangers to each other?

It did not take long before her constant seeking developed

into an unwholesome curiosity. Everything she saw or heard became the object of her exploration, and all too frequently she made use of highly improper methods in her quest. Her family was always on guard against her prying. Whenever they talked to each other they first looked around to see if she was within earshot. Sometimes her curiosity drove her to do such dreadful things that everyone around her became agitated and upset. But since she was no more than a child, bubbling over with song and vitality, they quickly forgave her antics and forgot about them. Not until she had reached the age of nineteen—it was the day after her mother died—did they begin to admit the truth to themselves.

Tall, slender, graceful, lovely to look at, with thick, jet-black curly hair that fell to her slim shoulders, she could usually be seen walking about by herself, her big eyes pensive. Always lonely and alone, even while she lived in a house full of people, she was forever studying them, questioning their motives. Her peers disliked her, tried to avoid her. In truth, they were more than a little afraid of her.

And not only her friends and family, but the whole town suddenly began to see her through different eyes, as though during the night an unknown spirit had flown across the rooftops, screaming down all the chimneys that tomorrow, if you did not view Shifra differently, you would be severely punished.

Evenings, when she customarily appeared outdoors, all eyes were upon her wherever she went. Through doors and windows people stared with half-a-face and two frightened, inquisitive eyes. Without looking around at anyone or anything, she would walk along, deep in thought, her back straight as a ramrod, her steps heavy and determined, but at the same time somehow uncertain. Her eyes darted ahead into all the corners. The shadow of a smile played skeptically upon her pale, pink, ever-so-slightly turned-up lips, so that you could never be certain whether she was about to laugh or cry. Her occasionally faltering stride created the impression that she was debating whether to walk farther or turn back.

Those who stared after her were unnerved by the big black shadow that followed deferentially behind her. They saw in it a sign of something mystical, arcane, ominous.

When she had increased the distance between them they would nod their tousled heads and wink at each other, as if to say, "That one will come to a bad end!"—and then they would be upset by their own presentiments.

As she walked farther and farther, the shadow at her feet grew larger and more terrifying, her face darker and more foreboding. And she continued to spin her raw, sorrowful thoughts, trying to reach a decision, so that if she really did succeed in finding the end of the tangled knot, she would be able to unravel the mystery.

2   Her mother's death affected her to the depths of her soul. It was not so much that she was no longer alive— she knew her mother was a sick and defeated woman, that her death was imminent. What distressed her much more, what caused her unbearable pain, was that her mother had taken with her into the deep, damp, dark grave the secret of why her daughter Shifra was such a stranger to the blood of her blood and the flesh of her flesh. Deep in her heart she knew that her mother, all her years, had spun the web of this terrible secret which she was afraid to reveal to the eyes of her husband and children.

Thirty long, onerous years her mother had lived with her father. Ten children she had borne him. Ten times she had risked her life. With a blissful smile on her exhausted face she had gladly offered herself up as hostage to the odious fangs of the Angel of Death. Six of her children she had buried; had seen six tiny graves chopped out of the cold earth. The grass had not yet grown on the first grave, the earth was still soft and fresh, the blood of her ailing, anguished heart had not yet ceased to drip, her eyes were still red and swollen, her breath heavy and labored, God had not yet forgiven her for the indignities she had suffered, when again new, ferocious winds had brought another affliction upon her bowed head.

Short and scrawny, worn out from constant drudgery and grief, twisted and old before her time, she lifted her emaciated arms, their skin dry and yellow, to heaven. She thanked God for her torments and beseeched Him to pour out all His wrath upon her head if her measure was not yet full; she would accept everything with love, so long as He shielded her children and her husband and kept them well and strong.

And it was this unfortunate, devoted old woman who found herself alone and forlorn. Her terrible pains remained hidden from those for whom her heart ached. A secret, a deep dark secret, lay buried in the depths of her soul, hidden away from everyone's eyes.

Shifra, when she was fourteen years old, became aware of all this. She began to notice that her mother was hiding something, something which nobody else was allowed to know. Her youthful mind worked very hard to discover what it could be. These and similar thoughts taxed her mind, oppressed her heart. Whenever she questioned her mother, she received no reply. When she grew a few years older she began to notice that everyone—everyone she knew—acted the same way: everyone had his own secret, everyone was lonely and alone; and she learned that not everything etched on a person's heart can be revealed, even to his own flesh and blood.

And the higher she raised the black curtain in order to
3   look more deeply at life, the more despairing she became, the deeper and more painful her wound. Often, when she found herself alone in the house, she would clasp her hands behind her head and with a muted, sorrowful voice cry out: "How shall I ever learn it? God in heaven, what can it be?"

She tried to ferret out her father's secret, to find out why he was so guarded in his words. Here, too, she failed. He never told the whole story about anything. No matter how much he said, he always held back something important. He was not afraid of his children, to be sure, but he was harboring something so secret that even his own family could not be trusted to know it.

More than once Shifra noticed that whenever one of their household was telling someone a quite ordinary thing, something already common knowledge to everyone, and there were no other members of the family present, it was a lively, colorful and fascinating story to hear. But should any one of them relate the same thing whenever another family member was listening, then the narrator kept looking around suspiciously and the story was boring, dull and tasteless. Why was that so? Really why? What is there in people that prevents them from telling the truth? Or what is it that compels them to lie?

She had once resolved that she would not let this bother her any longer. If this is how the world really is, so be it. And she consoled herself this way: either all human beings are essentially good, and when they say something, they mean it, and they never intentionally do another person harm; or conversely, there are no honest people in the world at all, one is worse than the other, and whenever someone puts his hand on his heart and swears, that's precisely when he's telling you the biggest lie.

For a little while afterward she felt better, more alive; she was able to joke, to dress up. She would suddenly fling her arms around members of the household, her laughter resounding wildly and emotionally and her bosom heaving. But this only alarmed her family more.

During that time she also had a few friendly words for Nochem, who had been coming to the house for almost three years, only because of her. And all this time he had been trying to work up the courage to have a serious talk with her, to tell her he loved her very much, that he understood her.

Nochem is tall, handsome, young, strong, with broad shoulders and hardened muscles. He has a good job. His blue eyes are warm, sympathetic. He says little but thinks a lot. And what he thinks about mostly is girls and how to win their hearts. What he finds most attractive are girls who are proud, even a little haughty. Culturally he is not too well advanced, nor is he overly intelligent. When the talk gets around to his weakness—women—he blushes. He cannot seem to rid himself of his small-town upbringing. When Shifra spoke those few amiable words to him he smiled good-naturedly and observed:

"It's going to be a nice day today after all!"

Shifra moved closer to him, took hold of his lapel and led him over to the sofa.

"Let's sit down for a while, Nochem."

Noticing that everyone in the room was staring at them, he put a little space between Shifra and himself. She placed her warm, dainty hand on his strong neck and said in an annoyed tone:

"Oh, Nochem, that's not nice! Why are you moving away from me? I know you'd really like to sit down beside me— why should you lie about it?"

Nochem's face reddened. His upper lip quivered. He inhaled a deep draught of air through his nostrils and defended himself: "I didn't move away from you at all!"

He felt her words sink into his heart. The pleasant warmth of her hand on his throat sent an unwonted tingle over his whole body.

"Do me a favor, Nochem. Tell me something—anything —and I'll just listen. But it must be something true. I want to hear how your voice sounds when you're telling the truth!"

She moved still closer to him and turned her right ear toward him, her eyes shining with warmth and affection. A curl of jet-black hair on either side of her pale face made it look saintly.

"You're insulting me, Shifra!" he protested. "I *always* tell the truth!"

Shifra did not even hear what he said. She stared straight ahead, her eyes wild, their gleam strangely reminiscent of madness.

Every day, every hour, every second, brought Shifra
4 new terrors, fresh disillusionments, deepening her despair and sharpening her torment.

On the day of her mother's funeral, the body—feet to the door—lay stretched out on the floor, covered with a grimy black cloth whose frayed edges were thickly matted with knots of white tallow that looked like buttons sewed on in careless disorder. The sight offended the eye. And at the height of their tragedy, Shifra's brothers and sisters ran around the house as though demented, looking in all the corners, as if they couldn't wait to get their hands on the paltry possessions left by the deceased.

Their pretext was false as man's life and suspicious as death: they were merely trying to get hold of these trifles because their deceased mother's memory was so very precious to them. Yet each tried to grab the more valuable items for himself, even if they were things their mother had never used.

Shifra studied her brothers and sisters, attempting to understand why they were doing this when they all knew that each of them was lying, that they didn't trust one another, that they were only trying to deceive each other. She had to know also whether her mother had really wanted to die, since she was constantly praying for her own death. Whenever an acquaintance or a neighbor died, she complained: why did God always take only those who weren't ready and let her live—she who was always begging for death? If that were true, then why did she scream so loudly for help when she was fatally stricken? Whom did she need to deceive, and why?

She had even asked her mother: "Mama, didn't you yourself often pray to God for this moment?" She had bent down and gazed deeply into her mother's glazed eyes, now bloodshot with infection, like the eyes of some poisoned creature.

"For shame, my child, for shame! Help me—"

Shifra's heart had tightened, her face had grown somber. Her own eyes had become bloodshot and a skeptical smile played on her pale lips, as though she were about to burst out laughing. She had run out of the bedroom and not returned until her mother lay dead. She had not even observed the seven days of mourning. When her friends warned her that she was violating a sacred and venerated custom, she had replied with hysterical laughter. In no time at all this latest peculiar behavior of hers was on the lips of the whole town, and from that time on, people began to fear her. . . .

5 Following close upon her mother's death, further blows began raining down on their household, but they fell heaviest on Shifra's lovely young head. The new disas-

ters and frustrations piled one atop the other, but an obscure, murky force gripped her, forced her to confront all these afflictions coldly and indifferently. She never even grimaced, as if she had been preparing herself for a long time, as though she knew in advance it was unavoidable, and was now pleased that the calamity had struck, because the agony of waiting for it to happen was much worse than the calamity itself.

At home and in the street she wandered solitary, her slender figure moving aimlessly about, her eyes sad, her thoughts inward. At home and in the street she walked always in a straight line, putting one foot deliberately in front of the other as though her gait itself was symbolic—one false step and she would plunge into the black, bottomless chasm.

In the street there were always young children who made a game out of trotting along beside her, mimicking her and calling her names. But she saw nothing, heard nothing. She continued spinning her raw, sorrowful thread of thought: she must come to a decision, so that if she ever found the edge of the tangled knot she would be able to unravel the mystery. . . .

Not until the children laughed and laughed and tugged at her skirt would she raise her head, startled as a doe, and then the children would flee, squealing. At such times her eyes were gentle, naive, full of longing, like those of an orphaned child. As soon as Shifra looked up, any grown-ups who had been watching would avert their eyes and walk away, abashed.

At last the troubles diminished somewhat, simply because there was no one left in the household to play the role of victim. They had all taken their turn in succumbing to a long and perilous illness. For many pain-filled nights and days they lay forgotten, dejected, bathing in their own colorless sweat. And one after the other, with excruciating effort, they sat up on their sickbeds, very slowly placed their feet on the floor, stood up on their shaking, sticklike legs, and fearfully learned to walk again, like babies taking their first steps.

The bitterness of suffering united Shifra with her father, sisters and brothers. They shared each other's agonies. They poured out their feelings of despondency, pain and hopelessness. But Shifra hoped that the happy time was beginning, that very soon she would learn why people were so distant and estranged from each other. It seemed to her that as soon as she learned the reason, then the solid, secret wall of suspicion between her brothers and sisters would crumble, fall and disappear.

6 That was the best time of Shifra's life. The least little incident that happened at home delighted her. She was like a child released into the outdoors at springtime. The eight large sullen rooms, the square, flat, blank walls which always seemed to Shifra to have their own secrets— even these walls now looked affable and friendly. No longer did they fill her with fear. And the old neglected furniture, all the household utensils, which always looked so lonely and desolate, so sad and dejected, because they knew all the family secrets and could share them with no one—all these forgotten objects now looked cheerful and content. They, too, had souls, Shifra felt, souls which were now happy for her, for the joyful upheaval in her life. Cleaning house, she paid close attention to each utensil, each object, so that none of them should feel neglected. Gathering straw by straw, grain by grain of sand, she untiringly built a structure in which she expected to dwell a long time. The deep wound in her young, tender heart began to heal, to close, to be covered over by a membrane as delicate as cobweb.

In a cheerful and happy mood, her eyes reflected a look of peace and serenity. Courageously she held her head high on her proud shoulders. Her mass of jet-black hair hung loose, tantalizing and exciting all the young fellows who came into the house. She looked at everyone warmly and lovingly. At the slightest provocation she laughed heartily, with a fresh, ringing laughter that worried the other members of the family and caused them to glance meaningfully at each other. The young men found her laughter strangely exhilarating, as though fine needles were lightly pricking their flesh. Nochem yearned to put his strong arms around her and cover her fragrant flower-body with fervid kisses.

Shifra knew that all the young men were infatuated with her. She could read it in their hot, impassioned glances, in their confusion, in their agitated movements. And this aroused in her a kind of desire to throw herself into a life of lust, to soak the lust into herself with all her powers, to gulp it thirstily, drink it down to the last dregs.

This new emotion that had flared up within her burned with a searing flame that penetrated to the marrow of her bones. Where this all-consuming longing had come from so suddenly, and why, she did not know, but it seethed within her, sang and raged and would not let her rest.

The very first time Nochem asked, she gave herself to him without even a why or wherefore. She did it mostly out of curiosity, but once the woman in her had been aroused, she became insatiable. This quiet young woman, always dreamy as the moon's halo, was suddenly transformed into an inferno that sprayed fire. It seemed as though she had always known what her dark fate would be, as though she had instinctively sensed what awaited her in the future. And since this was the first and last time she would enjoy life on earth, she must therefore throw herself into it body and soul, and at least for a brief moment lull her doubt and grief to sleep and drown her sinister despair in pleasure.

7

It happened unexpectedly, as though by accident. When Nochem entered her room she could see he was desperate to speak with her about something, but that he was having difficulty overcoming his shyness.

"Shifra—"

"Yes, Nochem?"

"Shifra—"

"What is it?"

"Shifra!" He moved toward her, took her face in his hands and began kissing her with wild abandon.

She could not see his face but she was certain that it had turned a fiery red, that he was not in control of himself, that this was the first time in his life he had ever kissed a woman with such passion. And this aroused her desire to an even greater pitch, made her more curious, awakened something within her that she did not recognize.

"Nochem, Nochem . . ."

"What is it, Shifrele?" Through his clenched teeth his voice was thick, feverish, fervent. He pressed his lips more insistently against her face.

"Nochem, Nochem—you'll knock me down! Not here—not here in this house!"

"*Shifrele, Shifrele—*"

"Please, Nochem, not here! Someone might come in!"

"Where shall we go, then? Let's run away from here! Shifrele, I love you so much—"

She kissed him long and passionately before she replied.

"I'll go wherever you wish, Nochem—but not here—"

He whispered something into her ear. She shook her head.

"Why not, sweetheart?" he pleaded.

"Because we couldn't stay there very long, and I want to be with you for a month—a whole month, you hear?"

He kissed her savagely, his whole body trembling. She did not utter another word, but only held him tighter.

That same day he rented a room in a nearby town and brought her there.

As soon as they were inside she locked the door, put the key in her pocket and began tearing off her clothes. When she was completely naked she demanded, "You, too, Nochem! Take off all your clothes!"

Her own voice, firm and peremptory, sounded unfamiliar to her.

As the moon slipped behind a cloud, the room grew dark. . . .

Not until he lay back on the bed, exhausted and spent, and other emotions began to return to him, did he realize that he was afraid of her. There was no hint of human love in her. She was like a famished wolf surrounded by enemies, an imperiled beast whose instinct drives him to attack, attack, up to the last desperate moment.

She threw herself upon him, kissed his hands, his feet, covered his mouth so that he could not speak, implored him not to deny her, demanded that he satisfy her every need.

Her lust was driving her mad.

Two days and two nights passed in this delirium of ecstasy. Tearfully he persuaded her at one point to eat something. And had she not spied the picture on the wall opposite the bed, on the second night, there is no telling how long she would have gone on this way.

She laughed, cried, laughed again, sank her teeth into her pillow. She could not find a place for herself. She lost all track of time.

At the end of the second night, Nochem got out of bed suddenly and pressed the light-switch. Startled, she sat bolt upright, and her eyes, darting this way and that, fell upon the picture on the wall.

She did not see the scene clearly, but that brief look was enough for the mute images, the copied shadows of human figures, to remind her of the big, noisy world outside, the false human beings with all their pettiness, and the mysterious secret which was so difficult for her to disentangle. As human thought returned to her she became aware of a gnawing weariness in all her limbs and she was smitten with shame.

Her languor, however, only served to inflame Nochem again. He turned off the light, leaped back upon the bed, and unrestrainedly covered her body with his lips. Coldly, without a word, she pushed him away, got out of bed and turned the light on again. The picture on the wall drew her like a magnet. Transfixed, she moved toward it and studied it. The longer she gazed at it, the deeper and sharper it burned itself into her brain.

The painting was quite ordinary, with no particular artistic merit; it was the subject matter that had riveted her attention:

Friday evening in an impoverished Jewish home. A woman is leaning forward over three Sabbath candles. Though her face is hidden in her hands, she appears to be weeping silently. Beside her, near the table, stands a young boy of nine or ten, trying to ascertain whether the woman is really crying. He is looking stealthily at his mother's hands, attempting to see between her fingers. He is a skeptic, he doesn't really believe. . . .

Studying the painting, Shifra shivered in fear. The boy on the canvas had become very dear to her, very close; she wanted to remove him from the picture, breathe life into him. Somehow she felt she had found a good friend in this lifeless image on the wall. Anger scorched her soul; the pain stabbing at her heart made her want to scream. Her emotions were agonizing, yet somehow pleasing, like scratching a healing wound. Agitated, humiliated, she picked up her clothes from the floor with shaking hands. Her whole body shivered, as if she were standing naked in a frosty gale. She had difficulty getting her clothes on. One sleeve of her undergarment, which had turned inside out, resisted all her efforts to right it. Impatiently she tossed the garment to the floor again. She pulled on her skirt and reached for her stockings, but could not find them. Grimacing in pain, she forced her bare feet into her shoes.

Standing there in her petticoat, with her unbuttoned shoes on her bare feet, with her unkempt black braids hanging untidily down her naked shoulders, she presented such a disturbed appearance that Nochem cried out in alarm.

"What's wrong, Shifra?"

"Didn't you notice that painting over there?" she demanded.

"What painting? What about it?" He put his hand on her soft, weary shoulder. "What's wrong with you? Get dressed, Shifra!"

Their shadows on the wall seemed to be contending.

"Nochem, what sensation do you feel when you put your hand on my body?"

"What?" He did not even understand her question.

He turned another light on. Their shadows vanished, but soon stole back onto another wall.

He helped her put her clothes on. Staring at the painting across the room, she grinned foolishly.

"Do you really love me, Nochem?" she asked abruptly.

He looked at her blankly for a moment. "Certainly I do!"

"I'd like very much to believe you."

"But?"

"It must be a wonderful feeling, to be able to believe—"

He nodded.

"Tell me, Nochem, do you ever believe what anyone says to you? But don't humor me!"

"I believe *you*, don't I?"

She had no answer to that.

"Shifra, let's stay here for the whole month—"

"And after the month is over you'll do the same thing with another woman?"

"How can you say such a thing, Shifra?"

She burst into frenzied laughter. Then her face grew angry, morose. Her eyes, red and sleepless, kept opening and closing; when they were open, the pupils seemed to be sinking into a white sea.

"What has happened to you today, Shifra?" he cried. His question was full of fear. "Let's get away from this place!"

But they stayed two more days. At every opportunity she looked at the painting. It was never out of her mind. As time passed, she grew calmer, almost serene. Again she became thoughtful; with her hands clasped behind her head she paced back and forth pensively across the room for long periods of time.

After they returned home, he came to visit her every day. She was not the least bit embarrassed. It did not bother her that people stared or gossiped.

Thus the gray days stretched into weeks and months. One evening, when they were alone in her room, they heard suspicious footsteps outside the door. He jumped away from her in alarm. She smiled ironically and shook her head. The big shadow on the floor rocked bizarrely.

"What's the matter, Nochem? What are you afraid of?" Her voice was ice.

He said nothing.

"Why don't you answer me? Why am I not afraid and you are?"

"I no longer understand you, Shifra. You've become such a stranger to me that I'm beginning to be afraid of *you*. . . ."

A few days later, when they were together in her room, he suddenly blurted out, "I hate you, Shifra!"

"Maybe you're only imagining it—" she murmured. She wanted to tell him more. She wanted to say, "You can't hate me now, Nochem. Right below my heart I'm carrying the fruit of our love. . . ." But she didn't stop him. Let him go! Let him go!

It was too late, anyway. He had already run out of the room. The door had uttered a hoarse groan, as if it, too, a bloodless, fleshless block of wood, was also suffering.

Slowly, counting every step, she walked over to the window and leaned out; perhaps she could still catch a glimpse of hm, even from a distance. Too late. . . .

Her restless eyes brimming over, her lips clamped tight, she walked away from the window, humiliated. She sat down on a sofa.

"Maybe he's really mistaken," she said to herself, her heart full of bitterness. "Maybe he only imagines it. . . ."

From that moment on she had nothing at all to do with him, did not even speak to him. They avoided being in the same room together. Out of their whole relationship it was the trivial things that had most deeply etched themselves into her memory, and they were never out of her mind. Everything else had dissolved, vanished in a vague, shifting vapor.

She recalled, for example, that whenever the young hired man had brought a tray of food into their room, he couldn't keep his eyes off her as he smiled ever so faintly but knowingly. Nochem was always careful not to let his eyes meet the young man's. Why? Why was she not ashamed to return his stare? Why was she able to give him orders in such a strong, confident tone?

These unimportant details, and others like them, stayed in her mind, though she would have much preferred to forget them. . . .

8 So imperceptibly that she hardly noticed it herself, the familiar feelings of despair and skepticism began to reassert themselves in Shifra's life. Unceasingly, the mys-

tery hovered before her eyes. Again she was obsessed with the desire to solve it once and for all. Again her family was on guard against her strange behavior. In the street, people shook their heads as they watched her. Brides stopped inviting her to their weddings. A rumor spread that wherever she appeared, disaster was close behind. If she happened to pass to and fro outside a house, the people inside would turn a shoe upside down or stick a knife into the ground to ward off the evil eye.

On one occasion, when she had been invited to a wedding, the whole celebration was disrupted as people moved away from her and she was left sitting all alone at a big table, surrounded by empty chairs. Shifra wondered whether the bride really believed that the groom loved her. Whenever she noticed wives or husbands enjoying themselves she tried to learn whether both sides were present. Often it turned out that the wife and husband were at separate tables. Then she watched them closely when they were sitting together—were they as vivacious as when they were apart?

Once more, difficult days set in for Shifra, difficult days, weeks, months. She grew to dislike her relatives more than ever, yet she still sought out opportunities to talk with them. The more they talked, the more certain she was that they were lying; and the more they lied, the more she felt a need to speak with them.

But as the signs of the new life growing inside her became unmistakable, Shifra rose higher in her own esteem. Below her heart a human being was being created, and she would be the absolute master of it. It would be made of her own flesh and blood, warmed beneath her breast and imbued with her spirit. As soon as it understood human speech, she would tell the child the whole truth, including how it had come to be born. She would hide nothing from her child. She would raise it to be without secrets, without mysteries. Let its soul be pure and translucent.

With these thoughts in her head, her still slender figure became even more erect, her bearing more proud. Her pensive eyes, whose colors changed with her thoughts, gazed wistfully into the distance, into other worlds, where there was neither night nor hidden secrets. A spirit was growing within her, however, a spirit that was itself full of mystery. Even a stranger seeing her for the first time could have detected that new lines were being engraved in her countenance, that even her bodily movements were somehow different.

Intuitively she was protecting herself from something, but she herself could not discern what it was. Nor did she even notice that the family was again keeping tabs on her. And when her sister asked, "Shifra, how many months have you been clean?" she did not even feel she was lying when she replied, "Same as usual! Why do you ask?"

Unbeknownst to herself she again fell into that state of painful doubt tinged with hope. Again she began spying on everyone within her circle, studying every step they took. She became so familiar with their idiosyncracies and their manner of thinking that very often she was able to predict how they would reply to a question or how they would react in any given situation.

Often it seemed to her that she already knew how to start unraveling the knot; that if she learned just a little more, it would all become clear to her. And she felt certain that this would happen only at a time of great misfortune, because by now she knew that at such critical times people are more emotional and therefore more truthful, and that it would be much easier to get to the bottom of the mystery. She must find out, she must know: Why are people so distant and estranged from one another? Why, when two individuals join together and—of their own volition—give life to a third human being—why, even then, does a deep, obscure, invisible barrier rise between them? She was therefore less disturbed now by all the troubles and afflictions that again began descending upon their household like falling rocks. She hoped that finally, finally, she would reach her goal and solve the mystery.

And her forebodings came to pass. Just as fire engulfs a haystack and consumes it, so tragedy engulfed the entire household and turned it to ash.

First her sister's father-in-law cut his own throat, with the same ritual-slaughterer's knife he had used on the chickens. And when Shifra watched Motl, her sister's husband, and saw the odd gleam in his eyes as he examined the knife, the thought blazed up in her head—as clearly as though someone had whispered it into her ear—that one day soon he would do the same thing his father had done.

She was so certain of its inevitability that she did not even feel it necessary to talk to her sister about it, or for that matter, with Motl himself, since it was so self-evident that he had no other way out. A consumptive, he had not worked for three years. His wife's earnings, though she worked day and night, were insufficient to maintain their own little family, and the result was constant bickering. Her relatives grumbled that her husband and children were weights around their necks and prayed for the day they would be rid of them. The only thing that puzzled Shifra was why he had not done it a long time ago. . . .

9 On this particular evening Motl asked Gitl to put clean linen on their bed. She promptly complied. When he got into bed, Shifra felt—no, she knew—that this was the last time he would sleep in that bed, or any other bed. All skin and bones, his chest sunken, he lay there staring out of bulging, wary eyes, his forehead bathed in sweat. A dark brown streak, like the mark of a whip, ran across the middle of his nose. His scrawny arms, on which the yellow skin hung as though it didn't belong there, lay stretched out on the blanket, motionless, dead. The room grew darker and darker, the shadow on the wall beside him larger and larger, as if it were the Angel of Death himself.

All of a sudden Motl sat up and called Gitl's name in a voice strangely cheerful. His eyes sparkled with that glint of certitude which bespeaks a firm determination to carry out a decision made after a long struggle. Gitl entered the room and put her toilworn hand on his dark, damp forehead:

"What can I get you, sweetheart?"

"Nothing. I want to talk with you, Gitl. Listen—" His next words were smothered by a coughing spell.

Gitl sat down beside him on the bed.

"Don't excite yourself, Motl. You know it's not good for you."

"Listen to me, Gitl. I have a feeling that—that my time has come—"

Gitl's hand dropped helplessly from his shoulder onto the pillow. She could no longer see him clearly for the tears in her eyes.

In a droning, dispirited monotone they talked for a long time. Stung by his admonition that she be a good mother to their daughters, she could only sob in reply.

Shifra, eavesdropping on their conversation outside the door, decided that as soon as Gitl left the room, she would hurry in and tell Motl that she knew what was in his mind and that he was doing the right thing. She would persuade him to tell her what was in his heart and promise not to betray a word of it to anyone. With morbid impatience she could hardly wait for that joyous moment when she and the dying Motl were alone.

But the instant Gitl left, Motl got out of bed and locked the door.

Thwarted, Shifra examined the door from her side. There must be a way for her to see inside that room. On her knees, she finally found a crack between two boards in the lower part of the door. She put her eye to it. Yes, thank goodness, Motl was in her line of vision.

She watched him sit up, take the knife from underneath his pillow and study it intently on all sides, as if he were concerned about its ritual purity. The faint smile on his lips was laden with meaning. Despite herself, Shifra moaned as Motl's right hand, with a swift, sudden slash, ran the knife across his throat. He fell back onto the pillow, his arms waving in the air as if they were fighting off an adversary. Then they dropped with a thud across his narrow chest. Only once did he try to raise them, but his strength had ebbed so quickly that his fingers could no longer even grip the knife.

When the blood had soaked through the pillow beneath his head and begun to drip onto the floor, and a red, serpentine trail curled away from the bed, Shifra, dancing up and down, began screaming *"Mazl-tov! Mazl-tov!"*

Terror-stricken, Gitl came running.

"What's wrong? Is he calling me?"

"Yes, he's calling you—hurry!" Shifra's laugh was that of a maniac, wild and unearthly.

Everyone in the house came running. Breathlessly, in a paroxysm of laughter, Shifra gestured with her head toward Motl's room. Gitl rushed to the door, then turned around, panic-stricken. She looked dumbly at Shifra, but Shifra's only response was an eerie, insane laugh that froze the blood of all who heard it.

"Shifra!" her father finally demanded. "What are you laughing at?" His voice was that of an old, forgotten man, but it portended something awesome.

"Answer him!" Shifra's sister ordered.

Shifra only laughed louder.

"It's the devil in her that's laughing!" Gitl cried. "Shifra! Why is the door locked?"

"He killed himself!" Shifra shrieked. "Motl—"

"Madwoman! Stop babbling!"

They all hurled themselves at the locked door, but it held fast.

"Look—" Shifra laughed. "Look here, through this crack—"

Gitl was the first to put her eye to the door. She leaped back with a horrifying scream.

Finally they broke down the door. As it gave way, the old man fell to the floor, slipping in the pool of blood that was flowing from the suicide's veins. . . .

10 The dreadful news traveled through the town like an enraged storm wind. Hundreds of people, young and old, pressed against the house, avid to set eyes on the extraordinary corpse behind the door.

Eighteen gruesome, ghastly hours passed before the deceased was laid in his grave. Those who came to pay their last respects wept, lamented the harrowing ordeal of the young widow and the orphaned little girls. But beyond all else, they enumerated the virtues of the deceased. Everyone lauded him to the skies. Not one person had an unkind word to say about him. Even those who had not known him, who had never set eyes on him, had only good words to say about him. Each one had something to praise about Motl, whether he believed it or not. And when the widow Gitl appeared, the lies flowed thicker and faster.

Shifra, her face grim, her arms folded rebelliously, her eyes glistening with grief and disquiet, stood by, murmuring to herself, "Lies! Lies! All lies!"

And when her sisters and brothers sat down on the ground at the head of the deceased, begging forgiveness from him and reminding him that he alone now knew the truth—that he had always been dear to them, that they had never dishonored him, that it had been a privilege for them to serve him in his final hours, that he had never been a burden to any of them— then Shifra's face contorted with disgust and she began making grotesque gestures. When she finally spoke, her voice was hollow and ghostlike:

"Motl, why are you silent? How can you bear it? Tell them all to stop lying!"

The mourners shuddered as if they were really afraid the corpse would come to life and start speaking.

"She's a lunatic!" someone proclaimed. Those who stood near Shifra edged away. When she took a step forward, they all jumped. Her voice, flat and expressionless, seemed to come from the grave.

"Gitl's father-in-law was the perfect candidate to be number one. Then it was Motl's turn. Now it's her turn. Next, it will be his—" She pointed to Gitl, then to her father.

All eyes opened wide in horror.

"Pour cold water on her!"

"Get her out of here! She's raving! Look at her!"

"Take her to a doctor, to the madhouse!"

Shifra ran out into the street talking to Motl, reproaching him for taking the secret with him into the deep, dark grave. . . .

One by one their neighbors moved away. A rumor spread that Shifra had a curse on her, that she was a demon, a witch, that she would bring bad luck and disaster to anyone whose life she touched. They would all join forces and kill her. At least have her put away. The rumor came to Shifra's ears, too, but it was of no concern to her. She continued to wander about, lost in thought, sullen, grim-visaged, talking to herself. Whenever she came upon a group of children playing in the street she attached herself to them with questions. Parents began to worry about what she was telling their children. A new rumor spread: children that she spoke to would die a mysterious death. After a while, after people kept driving her away again and again, Shifra no longer appeared in the street. And no one knew where she had vanished.

Outside the town, in a ditch near the graveyard, she had found a place of refuge. Every morning she would steal into the cemetery and slink from headstone to headstone, begging the graves to entrust their secret to her, swearing that she would never reveal a word to anyone else.

On the evening before *Tisha b'Av* she knocked at the gravedigger's window, screaming hysterically:

"Now I know! I have solved the mystery!"

The sound of her voice echoed among the graves like the call of a living soul lost among the silent dead....

Family Life: A Chapter

MEYLEKH AWOKE at five o'clock as usual, got out of bed and began reciting the morning prayers. Still saying the prayers, he went into the kitchen and stopped before a little cupboard that had lost both its legs. One side of it rested on two red bricks; the other on a thick log from a birch tree. He had given orders that on no account should the log be moved. On more than one occasion, when Fradel was down to her last piece of firewood, she had cast her eye on that big log. But Meylekh had specifically warned her: Let it lie there. The time would come, he said, when they would really need it, and then it would be a godsend, like found money.

He gave the log a little push with his foot; let it not stick out so much and be a temptation. Opening both doors of the cupboard, he sat down and picked through everything that lay inside; he counted the sugar cubes and the onions, measured the loaf of bread, opened the tea chest, shook it, shut it again, and put it back in its place. Leaving the closet open, he moved over to the kitchen table, pulled out the drawer and began inspecting its contents. All this he did slowly, deliberately, but almost absentmindedly.

Scraping together several flyspecked sugar cubes that had

already been bitten into, he blew the dust off them, and as he arranged them on the table, swore under his breath. Then he put his hand into the drawer again, found a few loose beans that had been lying there for who knows how long. One bean, stubbornly refusing to come out of its hiding place between two boards, only made him more determined to get it out. But the longer he dug at it with his knife, the deeper it embedded itself. Finally he uttered such a loud, exasperated oath that he woke up his wife.

"What are you making such a fuss about there?" she called from the bedroom. "You want to wake up the children, too? Have you fixed such a good breakfast for them? I'm happier when they're asleep. You murderer! Not an ounce of pity! All night long the baby has been sucking the life out of me. Now that I'm finally able to get a little sleep he even begrudges me that!"

Her tirade only made Meylekh angrier. His swearing became more vindictive. "I wish I was rid of the whole lot of you! Soon I'll have to go begging in the houses on account of you! Look how they waste good food! The Czar's pantry wouldn't be enough for you! Parasites! Don't give a damn about me! Work like a dog, roast in the sun all day long—and they loaf around here—"

"Who's wasting food? What food? Wretch! You're in one of your snooping moods again?"

"Look how much sugar I took out of the drawer! And all these beans lying around loose!"

"The sugar is not yours, it's Dovidl's!"

"Tell that to your grandmother! You could make a nice lunch out of it today!"

"Why don't you keep it all under lock and key? You and your valuable property!"

"Maybe I'll just do that! It's the only way to keep it safe from you!"

"Keep what safe from me, you monster? It's all for you and your little bastards!"

A terrible thought went through Fradel's head: It would be a lot worse if he knew the truth! My God, what a life she led! Never hearing a kind word. All she ever heard all day and night was screaming and swearing! True, she was a grievous sinner herself—she shouldn't be allowed into a Jewish home. Stoning is what she deserved. But as God was her witness, if her husband weren't such a mean, cruel man it might never have come to this. . . . Other wives quarrel and fight over nothing—give them money for delicacies, buy them silk kerchiefs, combs and watches, hire a servant for them. But such things never even entered her mind. All she ever wanted was that he be a *mentsh*.

A sigh tore out of the depths of her soul. . . .

Meanwhile, Meylekh had taken off his *tallis*-and-*tefillin* and finished his tea. He cut several slices of bread for the children, and on each slice laid two cubes of sugar. The remainder he wrapped up and put back into the drawer. For a moment he stood there absently, then took out another piece of sugar and left it on the table for his four-year-old Chaiml, who was ailing. As he did so, he muttered: "Never mind, her tea will be sweet enough with only two lumps."

After a few more barbs at his wife, Meylekh got ready to leave—it was already a quarter to six.

From a hook on the wall he took down his long black gabardine, which had been covered by a long white sheet. Slowly and methodically he put it on. As he stared at his shoes, which couldn't take even one more patch, he said to himself: "If only I can manage to sell some wood today without Chaim Greenberg knowing it, the first thing I'll buy is a new pair of shoes. All these years I've worked in his lumberyard and I can't even afford . . ." He took off his cap, blew the dust off it vigorously, wiped the peak with the sleeve of his gabardine, examined himself in the mirror, brushed the crumbs off his beard, sighed, and started toward the door.

"Listen, Your Excellency," Fradel called after him, her tone a bit milder. "Will you be home for supper? If so, you'd better leave me a little money. There isn't a groshn in the house."

Meylekh noted the softening in her tone. Turning back toward the bedroom, he replied almost affably, "I'll be home earlier today and bring you some money."

As soon as he left, Fradel went to see if he had eaten anything with his tea. When she saw that he had, she felt a little

better, but still not completely at ease. She reproached herself
for berating him. Why couldn't she control herself? How many
times she had resolved not to let herself be provoked by him,
yet now she had done it again. The irony of it did not escape
her. *She* was reprimanding *him*! *She* was acting the accuser!

She went to the sofa where her two young boys—one
four, the other six—were still asleep. She adjusted the pillow
under their heads, kissed them tenderly on their cold fore-
heads and covered them with the rags that served as blankets.
She drove away the flies, but opened a window to let in some
fresh air.

"If only Shloyme would come in right now!" she said to
herself as she went back into the bedroom, then immediately
regretted her own thoughts. Why did she miss him so? She
had grown so accustomed to his visits every morning that
whenever he was a little late she worried that he was losing
interest.

She loved to reminisce about the day she first told him
she loved him—and how they discovered that they had been
in love with each other for a long time, but neither one had
dared say anything! It had happened one morning when Meylekh was acting even more offensively than usual. He had
called her every name in the book, had threatened to drive her
out of the house, had even raised his hand to her. Why he was
carrying on this way she didn't begin to understand, but it
depressed her so much she thought of taking her own life.
Standing alone in her room, sunk in sinister thoughts, she did
not hear the front door open.

Suddenly, from behind her, two hands covered her eyes. A
pair of lips were kissing the back of her neck, her hair. She had
not immediately known who it was, but a fire had blazed up
within her. His kisses burned so sweetly, made her feel so
desired, that she knew she had been waiting for this all her
life—and was not even surprised that she didn't know who
the man was or why this was happening to her, of all people.
She wanted to seize the hot hands that were over her eyes, to
kiss them a thousand times, but she did not do so.

After a moment she twisted away. In truth, she would

much rather have stayed enfolded in those tender, insistent, arms for the rest of her days, but he himself had relaxed them and said:

"Freydele, now do whatever you wish with me. But it's not my fault. It was not I who did this. the stormy passion that has been building up inside me ever since I've known you simply took possession of me and I could no longer withstand it. . . ."

Why was he apologizing to her, she wondered. He had only followed his natural impulse—oh my, how could she even think such things? As she looked at him, a stream of hot tears gushed from her eyes.

He had come toward her, embraced her, spoken soothingly to her: "I'm the only one in the world who understands you, Freydele, the only one who knows what's in your heart. What can I do to make your life easier, to stop your tears? Tell me! Whatever you ask me to do I'll do—" His words were so caressing, so sweet, so full of love, that they went straight to her heart, intoxicated and bewitched her. His voice, his gestures, his movements, all became part of her. She felt as if she were being hypnotized, as if she could fall asleep for a long, long time, as long as he kept on speaking to her.

And then she heard a voice saying:

"Do whatever you want for me, do whatever you want *with* me. I am yours, all yours! Oh Shloyme, I have loved you for such a long time, but I had to smother my feelings for you—and you know why. . . ."

Shloyme had been waiting behind the fence for an hour. He would have gone into the house sooner, but didn't know whether Meylekh had left for work yet. Not that he couldn't have come in even with Meylekh there. But why do that? It would still have been indiscreet—what was he doing there so early in the morning?

But as soon as his brother-in-law left, Shloyme went straight to the house. He stopped outside a window and tapped on it lightly with his finger.

"Who is it?" Fradel asked, and without waiting for an answer she had run into the kitchen and opened the door for him.

They greeted each other with smiles of playful delight. He put his arms around her and pressed her sturdy body to his. Looking directly into his eyes, she told him what had happened that morning between her husband and herself.

"But who cares, let him do whatever he wants, and we'll do whatever we want," she concluded, and blushed at her own audacity. "Tell me the truth, Shloyme, do you love me as much as I love you?"

By way of reply he hugged her so tightly that she squealed.

"You'll break my ribs, Shloyme!"

"So what?" he grinned.

"Listen to me, Shloyme. But seriously, Sarah tells me that you're acting crazy again. Why are you starting up again? Two weeks ago, when I was at your house, you and she quarreled. Remember? And didn't you and I agree then that neither Meylekh nor Sarah would suffer because of—because of us? Why can't you be like me? Look, I'm a hundred times more considerate of Meylekh now than I ever was. Shloyme, if you want me to feel relaxed, be good to her. Do it for my sake. I know you're always so sorry afterward, it breaks your heart."

"Fradel, let's talk about it some other time—"

"No. I want you to give me your word now."

"I do. I promise," he smiled.

They went into the bedroom and their talk grew more intimate. She told him that yesterday Sarah had visited her with the children, that the children had played nicely together, that they all loved the baby, Chayele, and vied with each other to hold her. . . .

"What do you think, Shloyme, can they possibly know she's their sister?" she asked, looking for the answer in his eyes.

"Of course they know!" His smile now had an ironic twist.

She did not ask him anything else. She could not find the right words. For a few moments they stood silently, until the silence began to oppress them.

"Shloyme!"

"Yes?"

"One more question, but you've got to tell me the whole truth."

"What is it, Fradel?"

She shuffled nervously from one foot to the other and finally summoned up the strength to ask:

"Shloyme, why don't I ever see *you* kissing Chayele the same way you do your other children? Isn't she—"

"You're talking nonsense, Fradel!"

"Is it nonsense?" she pouted.

"It certainly is, and you know it. Mark my words."

"You and your clever words! You should have left them home!"

"Now you can explain something to *me*, Fradel! Why do you expect me to repeat the same words a thousand times?"

"Now who's talking nonsense? Why do I enjoy it so much to sit here and talk with you like this? Don't you feel the same way?"

"Let's discuss it some other time, Freydele."

"Don't call me Freydele, it won't help you."

"You're certainly acting very strangely! Why are you picking on me today?"

"Do you deserve better?"

Before he could respond, Chayele began to cry. It was her time to be fed. Fradel picked her up, began nursing her.

"Glutton! Just like your father! Always hungry! Here— eat!" she exclaimed in mock anger, but her tone was agitated, uneasy. Why didn't Shloyme ever really listen to her when she wanted to be serious about something?

He came closer, put his arms around her and the child. As he kissed her, he bit her lip. Her uneasiness turned to anger.

"Are you deliberately trying to hurt me? You'd never do that to Sarah!" She pulled away from him.

He was so ashamed of himself that his face grew pink, then red, then white, and he could not look her in the eye. She regretted her words, her anger, wanted to take him in her arms, too.

"Why do we keep tormenting each other like this?" she murmured through her tears. "Isn't it enough that the rest of the world will point a finger?"

Shloyme looked at her guiltily, not knowing how to mollify her. Like a simpleton, he stood there mute, watching a patch of sunlight steal into the room and settle on Fradel's shoulder. With each one of her sobs it trembled, danced, then leaped playfully from her shoulder to the combs in her hair, from her head down to her bare feet, then back up the wall, stretching out over the entire room. The sunbeams kissed the kitten dozing on the floor, skipped back to Fradel's breast and rested on the childish mouth tightening around the nipple.

"Precious little baby! Have you gone and caught cold? Don't get sick, my little one! You are my life, my only consolation. You may be superfluous to someone else, but not to me, never to me!"

Her words roused Shloyme from his fascination with the sunbeams. He realized they were meant for him, those words, and that he ought to respond to them somehow, if he wanted Fradel to forgive him.

"Chayele," he said to the baby, "tell your mother she is a silly woman, that you will be much cleverer than she and all her other children. . . ." He smiled, moved closer to Fradel, took her hand, and wordlessly led her over to the window.

Her eyes dropped and under them appeared delicate pink stains which spread further and further across her pale cheeks. But she did not protest, and followed him as though in a dream.

He took the baby out of her arms, laid it gently in the crib and put a teething ring in its hand. Then he turned and swept Fradel up in his arms.

She twined her arms around his neck and covered his face, his head, with searing kisses.

"Oh, Shloyme, Shloyme! What are you doing to me?" she whispered. "Don't torture me . . . I'm unhappy enough as it is!"

And burying her head in his chest, she sobbed for a long, long time. . . .

Troubles

YANKL ZAK, proprietor of an entire block of brick-and-stone houses and operator of a fleet of Jewish funeral coaches, stepped outdoors one morning and, as was his daily habit, sat down on the wooden bench in front of his home. Yankl was short and stocky, with pudgy fingers and watery eyes.

Most mornings, before he sat down to rest, he crossed the street, surveyed the length and breadth of his "estate" and rejoiced in his own phenomenal good fortune. His property (knock wood!) must be worth at least half a million rubles! He sighed. If only he had some work for his horses now, he might be able to buy up Stamm's building, which was opposite his, by autumn. A marvelous courtyard, with all the flats in livable condition, ready for tenants. The building itself was one thing, but the location—perfect! And such a bargain—ninety thousand rubles—cheap as dirt!

On this particular morning, agitated and upset by his troubles, Yankl did not cross the street to contemplate his possessions. Even before he sat down his thoughts were revolving around the sorry state of his current income and what might happen if another week passed and his horses still had not worked, God forbid. . . .

He caught himself. It was sinful of him to think this way; whenever his horses worked, it meant that somebody had died. But this did not distress him for very long. After all, he wasn't actually hoping that young people should die. On the contrary, it was better for him if only old people died, because no matter what the age of the deceased, he got his twelve rubles for the horses. So what difference did it make to him? In fact, he had to admit to himself that it was somehow more gratifying when his horses were carrying a man of wisdom and maturity. And for those why are dying, it matters little whether they live another week or another month. For him, however, in his line of business, it made a big difference indeed.

His head continued working on the problem, a problem which only a clever brain like his could grapple with, and was on the verge of a solution, when the few nips of brandy and the ample lunch he had just eaten—and more than anything else the warm, caressing rays of the sun stealing in through the two acacia trees swaying in front of his house—all of this together overpowered him, and he dozed. . . .

"Reb Yankl, do me a special favor and send the horses to me first," pleaded Sholem Watchmaker. "The body has been lying here since yesterday afternoon!"

"I can't send them specially to you, don't you understand that? You have to wait your turn!"

"But Reb Yankl, we're such old friends. . . ."

"Yankl, you promised to take the child away at dawn— and now it's already eleven o'clock!"

"Go away, Leybl, I don't have time for you to cry on my shoulder!"

"Reb Yankl, don't send the horses anywhere else today!" Big Munye, who works for Yankl Zak, comes running over, all out of breath. "The *shammes* says he already has eleven bodies and there are two more waiting in the hospital. You can't let an old Jewish scholar lie around because of some young puppy—isn't that right?"

"Certainly, certainly!" Yankl agrees in his rasping voice as he melts with pleasure. "Munya, where the hell do you always disappear to when I need you? Run over to the smithy right away. Tell the boys to put bands on the two spare carts and shoe the extra horses. Maybe God is finally showing his compassion and I'll have enough work this season."

"Reb Yaakov, please send the horses for my mother-in-law," begs Melech Moneylender.

"I can't do it now, Reb Melech! On my word of honor. There are eleven ahead of you!"

"That's no excuse! I'll give you an extra five rubles for the trip! And I'm not budging from this spot until you—"

"For five stinkin' rubles I can't make a special trip for anybody! What kind of a fool do you take me for?"

Yankl feels that he is shouting so loudly his lungs are bursting. . . .

"Reb Yankl! Reb Yankl! Wake up! What are you hollering about?"

His neighbor is shaking him.

"I can't do it! I can't do it!" Yankl continues to shout, still arguing with Melech Moneylender.

"What can't you do?" the neighbor insists.

Yankl shakes his head, scratches himself, opens his eyes. Standing before him is Shmuel Feinstein, round and squat as a barrel. Reb Shmuel also owns an apartment building. In addition, the rumor is that he runs most of the shady enterprises in the town.

"What can't you do and why were you hollering? Must have been having a bad dream, eh, Reb Yankl?"

"Et, it was nothing—" Yankl mutters, bewildered and embarrassed.

"You can't fool me, Yankl! You must've been calling that juicy Natalia in your dream and she didn't come so quickly. . . ."

"Ai, Reb Shmuel, when will you grow up? You're almost sixty and you still think about such nonsense?"

"You call that nonsense? Ha-ha-ha—" Shmuel is almost convulsed with laughter.

"Ai, Reb Shmuel, if you only knew how much trouble I'm having now, you'd understand why such nonsense doesn't even enter my head. . . ."

"Your troubles can't be any worse than mine," smiles the neighbor.

"How do you know? You can't even understand the problems I have in my business."

"I do understand, I do, believe me. . . ."

"For the last six weeks my horses haven't done a day's work! Six weeks! You understand what that means?"

"Yes, I understand," sighs Reb Shmuel, his expression growing more serious. "Certainly I understand! But it's nine weeks since *my* horses have worked. Twice I've had to use the rent collections, instead of taking them right to the bank. And I've had my eye on a good piece of property recently—a real bargain—but I haven't been able to buy it."

Yankl Zak's heart stopped. Was his neighbor going to snatch Stamm's building right out of his fingers?

"Still," continued Reb Shmuel, "I can laugh about it. As the peasant says, 'If I had enough to eat, I'd be happy as a bull in heat!' Ai, brother, I haven't had such a bad season in a long time. Nine weeks, you understand? But listen, Reb Yankl, do you have any good whiskey in your cellar? Just a few drops and we'll—if you don't have any, come over to my place—"

"Why shouldn't I have a bottle?" Yankl protested indignantly. "Things aren't that bad yet, God forbid. Let's both drown our troubles!"

The two neighbors went indoors. Behind their backs they referred to each other by the same names as did the rest of the townsfolk—Yankele Fool, Shmuelke Lecher, etc. But face to face they treated each other with the utmost respect.

"Miriam, put something on the table right away for me and my friend Reb Shmuel! I'll go for the schnapps myself." In a moment he was back with two bottles.

"What do you say to some herring and onions in vinegar before we start the meal, Reb Shmuel?"

"Fine! You convinced me!"

They sat down to eat.

Yankl unbuttoned his jacket. (*Let him look at my new gold chain, let it blind him a little!*)

Shmuel took out his gold cigar case and laid it on the table. (*Here, you schmuck, eat your heart out!*)

"*L'chayim*, Reb Shmuel!"

"*L'chayim*, Reb Yankl!"

As he downed his fourth glass, Yankl said, "Ai, Reb Shmuel, such a good summer I expected this year. At worst, I thought, it would be like last year, or the one before. But the season I'm having now—may God protect me! I've never seen anything like it! With you, if something happens to one of your animals, at least you get something for the hide, for the bones, for the tallow. In my case, there's no hide, no bones, nothing at all. I only get paid when the horses work. If God helps and they work three-four times a day, fine. But if they work only once a day? Well, even once is better than nothing at all. Not that I make anything on it, but it covers expenses— for the smithy and the fodder and a few other things. Forget about my profit. But now it's six weeks—"

"Well, Reb Yankl, don't worry yourself sick. God will help. Soon there will be work for you and for me, too, I can feel it in my bones. In the meantime, let's drink to our troubles!"

"I can't—I don't have any more room—" He groaned as he patted his stomach.

"Eh, Reb Yankl, you really *are* getting old! Six tiny glasses —is that all you can handle?"

"Six, you say? I had four shots with my breakfast before I even stepped out of the house!"

"Good for you! Reb Yankl, let's drink to better times!"

"Don't fill mine all the way to the top—"

"Why not? Don't be a sissy—"

"*L'chayim*, Reb Shmuel! May God help you with a hundred and sixty hides a week, two hundred pounds of tallow and three hundred loads of bones!"

"From your mouth to His ears! And may your horses work ten times a day!"

"I hope so!" Yankl prayed fervently, touched by such a generous, neighborly wish.

The two worried men moved a little bit closer, gulped their whisky and kissed each other tearfully.

"Ai, if only all our wishes would come true," Yankl mumbled, licking his lips like a cat. With great effort he opened his eyes, which had begun to droop after his seventh glass. He opened his mouth, feeling an urge to pour out his bitter heart to his good friend Feinstein. He tried to stand up to shake his hand but, to his great surprise, he could not lift himself out of his chair. He decided to stay where he was.

"You understand, Reb Shmuel—my troubles—" He could not get the next word past his tongue, which had suddenly grown too big for his mouth. He spit and tried again. This time his tongue wouldn't stop.

"They say, Reb Shmuel—they say that when a man can't make a living, he at least get some pleasure out of his wife and children. Thank God, I don't have that, either. For my Miriam, my new droshky isn't fancy enough—she must have a carriage with two horses and a coachman, otherwise she won't even step into it. . . . I try to argue with her—what do we need it for, just to show off for the neighbors? You think she listens to me? Not on your life! She's always got to have her own way. . . . And if that's not enough, now my Volodya wants his own buggy, too, on rubber wheels, and two ponies that will burn up the road. He doesn't want to disgrace me, he says—"

"You think you're—you're the only one with—with troubles?" Shmuel interrupted, his voice thick. "But let's forget it today, let's have one more drop for better times, for a good season—the season is only beginning—"

"I know that, Reb Shmuelik—you think I don't know the season is only beginning? Yankl Zak, who became a builder with a mere thousand rubles in his pocket and now owns a whole block of houses—Yankl Zak knows everything. You want to guess how much I'm worth, Reb Shmuel? I'll be all right as long as my head works—this one." (He slapped his forehead to indicate what head he meant.) "My wish for you is that you have three hundred hides a week. And for myself, that people should keep on croaking, ha-ha!"

"Keep on croaking, right," echoed Shmuel Feinstein in his sleep. He tried to raise his head from the table, but it fell back with a thump.

And Yankl Zak can't remember how he came to be asleep on the plush sofa with his feet propped up on a chair. . . .

Incomprehensible

(A LETTER)

As soon as I stepped off the train and started walking through the narrow, crooked streets leading to the center of this town I got the feeling that I would enjoy my vacation here as much as I did last summer in Odessa.

You'll remember that in Odessa I almost went crazy with all the noise and hullabaloo. Here, on the other hand, in this congealed and silent shtetl, one quickly becomes bored to distraction. But don't think the people here have no thoughts in their heads. On the contrary. This little town possesses its own six or seven thousand two-legged animals, and each animal takes full advantage of every opportunity to bark and howl as loud as possible in order to be noticed.

And the clothing they wear! I suspect that if they could but stand the heat they would put on all the clothing they own at one time. Especially the women. They're simply impossible. If you would see the earrings they indulge themselves in you'd be scared out of your wits. Each earring weighs half a pound, without exaggeration. But life here is so humdrum, so routine, that it practically slumbers under a thick blanket of mildew.

More than once it occurred to me to go out into the middle of the marketplace and scream with all my might, maybe I could at least stir up the stagnant water a bit.

Fortunately for me, I did not succumb to this temptation. No doubt they would have dragged me straight to the madhouse.

So listen. I looked around and soon realized that sitting around and grumbling was going to get me nowhere, because the silence here is so infectious that it gets into your bloodstream. And that was something I wanted to avoid at all costs! So I went out and explored the town, looking for somebody who was still alive. Well, my friend, you know the old maxim—if you look for something hard enough, you're sure to find it!

What shall I tell you, brother? Accidentally I walked into a little world that consists of only three two-story houses, but you see a lot more life there than in all the rest of the town put together.

I don't know what the place looks like by day, but at night, things are really lively there. Outside of each house stand two poles, each one with a bright light—almost too bright.

This neighborhood, which is at the outskirts of the city, is separated from the main streets by a high, steep hill, so that if you didn't know about it, you'd never imagine that on the other side of the hill—which reaches almost to the sky and drops sharply on the other side—you would never in your life imagine that people live there.

Well, why should I make a short story long? In one of those houses I sat for two solid hours and couldn't wait any longer, that's how busy they were.

So I left.

A few steps from the house a young boy ran over to me. "Why go in there?" he said to me in a loud whisper. "Come with me and I'll show you a better place—and cheaper, too!"

I followed him.

First he led me along a twisting, circuitous path. Then the path dropped so precipitously that we had to run to stay on our feet. He ran ahead of me, turning his head every few moments to see whether I was still behind him. In this way we got to a house with a thatched roof and a wooden porch with two red posts.

Leaving me standing on the porch, he dashed into the house. A few seconds later the door opened and an old graybeard stuck his head out. He looked me up and down and invited me in.

I followed him.

In the hallway I tripped over a loose floorboard. This upset the old man so much that he begged my pardon and angrily cursed out the carpenter for not coming to repair the board as he had promised.

As we entered a large anteroom, he showed me to a chair and asked me softly:

"One ruble, or three?"

"Three!" I replied, not knowing exactly what the difference would be.

He excused himself politely and left the room. In a moment two women appeared, one about thirty, I'd guess, the other no more than fifteen. The older one stared at me out of a pair of large, hostile eyes.

The two women immediately began arguing about where to take me.

The young girl stamped her foot and practically shouted: "I say he goes to Manya! I know what I'm talking about!"

I sat and waited for them to settle the argument, but in my mind I already agreed with the younger one because of her innocent yet faintly cynical look and the saucy, winsome smile struggling at the corners of her mouth. In any case, having won the contest, she took me by the hand and led me to a door, then turned and left. For a few seconds I hesitated before that door, summoning up the courage to open it.

Inside the room, a young woman of about twenty sat at the window, apparently deep in thought. As I entered, she jumped, then measured me from head to toe with a frown. But that was only momentary. She quickly recovered herself and her eyes became friendly though dispassionate.

My attention was instantly caught by pictures of several classical Yiddish writers hanging on the wall above her table, which was covered by a green cloth. On one side of the room stood a new trunk with metal trimming.

"Excuse me!" I apologized. "I didn't mean to startle you."

She nodded and pointed to the trunk, the only other place in the room to sit down. I sat. She bent down and pulled a Japanese screen from underneath the bed. She unfolded it, stepped behind it for a moment and then said matter-of-factly:

"You may come in now."

As I did so I noticed that she had draped kerchiefs over the pictures on the wall, as well as over the few books lying on the table.

I handed her five rubles. She did not thank me.

Three of the bills she put into one drawer, two in another.

"The five are for you," I said. "I already paid him."

"I know. I would give him all five of these, too, he's such a poor man. But I need the money to help a friend of mine— she's studying to be a midwife."

I could not contain myself. "What *are* you doing in a place like this?" I blurted out.

She gave me a sharp glance but did not answer. Her eyes went through me like spears.

"I should think you could find some other occupation," I said, trying to soften my involuntary outburst, but only making it worse.

"Thanks very much!" she retorted. "What are *you* doing in a place like this?"

Those were the last words she spoke to me. When I awoke at six in the morning she was fully dressed and sitting on the trunk, reading a book by Peretz. The pictures and the books were still covered.

Dear friend, maybe you understand that young woman? I must admit, to me she was utterly incomprehensible. . . .

In a Dream

Every evening Itsik came home from work toilworn and weary, but tonight he was even wearier than usual. All day long Leah's tears had haunted him. Wherever he turned he saw them. What made it worse was that he knew she was not to blame. And this only made him feel more contrite.

"A gangster has more pity than you!" Leah had chided him. He forced a crooked smile. How little she understood him, if she really thought him cruel. His lips twisted ruefully as he recalled every word she had uttered. Absently he put down the piece of goods he had been working on, pushed his shears to one side, leaned heavily on his right elbow and stared straight ahead, as if Leah were standing directly in front of him.

"What do you expect me to do? Why are you eating my heart out? Why?" Her tear-soaked words still rang in his ears. "I scrimp and save and work my fingers to the bone, trying to make ends meet on six dollars a week! How far can I stretch six dollars in such a household, with five growing children, God bless them? Seven mouths to feed, *k'n'hora*! What little I eat is enough for me, but what about you? You must have a bit of meat every day, otherwise you won't even have the strength to work."

"I'm not blaming you at all," he thought to himself. His bloodshot eyes filled up with tears of angry desperation. "And how bad she looks! A skeleton—all skin and bones! She can barely stand on her feet. And those mischievous kids—they don't let her alone for a minute. Not that she ever complains. But I must teach them a lesson. They must learn to obey her! No, I'd better not beat them—that would only make her feel worse. What I should do is apologize to her. We should agree never to quarrel again. Why should we fight? Do we hate each other, God forbid? I'll show her I'm not a cruel husband—for a week now I've been racking my brains: where can I get the money to buy her a new pair of shoes?"

But as usual he could actually tell her none of this—he had never been able to say what he felt.

Silently, wordlessly, she served him his supper, and silently, wordlessly, she began making up the beds. In silence he finished his meal, sighed deeply, and went to bed.

He dreamt.

He is rich, wealthy, a millionaire. He comes home every evening to a happy, contented wife. The children run joyfully to meet him, expecting the customary gifts.

He does not disappoint them. He distributes toys to each child, then sends them outdoors to play. He comes over to Leah, who is resplendent in a white silk blouse. He takes her hand, pinches her arm gently.

"What beautiful material!"

"Please! That hurts!"

"Whom? You—or the blouse?" He moves his hand higher along her arm.

"What is it with you today, Itsik? How come you're so cheerful?"

"Why not? Is there anything I need that I don't have, thank God? I'm a rich man. I have five wonderful children. And my wife isn't so bad-looking either!" He puts his arms around her, tries to kiss her. She turns her head from side to side, avoiding his lips.

He gets an idea. With his left foot he pulls over the easy chair that is behind him, plumps down in it and tries to pull her down onto his lap.

"Be careful, Itsik! You'll break the springs!"

"So what? We'll buy another one!"

"Stop it! Someone might come in! You left the door open. How will it look?"

"I know you, you little tease! You're trying to trick me into letting go your hand, so you can run away! Better come with me and we'll both lock the door!" He holds her hand tightly as they walk toward the door.

"You know, Leah my dear, how much clear profit we'll make this month?"

"How much?"

"Guess!"

"I'm not a fortune-teller!"

"Just a fortune hunter?" he laughs.

She grins, nods.

He puts his arms around her trimly corseted waist and hugs her tightly. "Give me a big kiss, my little fortune hunter!"

"No!" she protests.

"Then I won't tell you how much profit we earned!"

"Come on, Itsik, be a good boy and tell me!"

"First the kiss!"

"After you tell me!"

"No, right now!" He pulls her closer. She struggles a moment, then kisses him on the lips.

"For that—here! Count it!" He tosses a handful of paper money into her lap.

"Oh my! she cries gleefully.

"Say *k'n'hora*!"

She gathers up the bills, stuffs them into her bosom, embraces him. "Now are you satisfied?"

"Not completely!"

She takes his head in her hands, rumples his hair, pulls it down over his eyes, kisses him passionately.

For a few minutes they are both silent. Then Leah says:

"Do you remember, Itsik, once upon a time, long ago, how cruel you were to me? Oh, were you a terrible husband!" She rolls her eyes heavenward.

He puts his hand over her mouth, kisses her forehead. "Whatever made you think of that, all of a sudden?" He doesn't like to hear her mention that. He is ashamed to recall it. How was it possible? Why did he do it? Such a precious little wife! A jewel! His heart constricts with pity for her. Tomorrow he must buy her a potted palm, just like the one she admired so much in his partner's home. Yes, tomorrow he would get her a plant, even if it cost twenty-five dollars. He would not bring it home with him. He'd have it delivered, and he'd act as if he knew nothing about it. Leah would be so surprised, so happy. . . .

Clang! Damn that murderous alarm clock! Itsik shuddered, opened his eyes sleepily, didn't remember where he was. But then his glance fell upon the battered sofa his children slept on. It cleared his head. He sat up. Yes, it had been a dream. But a good dream. It would be very pleasant to slip back into it again. It was only five o'clock, he could get another hour's sleep if he skipped his bread and tea—he could live without it.

"Itsik! Itsik!" Leah was shaking him. He sat bolt upright, in a daze.

"What's wrong? What's wrong?"

"It's after eight!"

"Oh no!" he wailed. Dressing quickly, he ran out. No time now for tea.

"Good-*yontef*, capitalist!" his fellow workers greeted him. "Why so late? Nobody at home to wake you?"

"He's got a wife to do that!" someone laughed.

"A wife can ruin your life, eh, Itsik? Remember when you were single and free as a bird? But as soon as you take a wife you've got a load on your back! Might as well be buried alive!"

"Take it easy, Itsik! Don't be in such a rush to start work-

ing—the boss will dock you for two hours anyway. No joking,
Itsik, why didn't she wake you in time, your missus?"

"Why should she," retorted the bachelor. "You think
that's all they have to think about, those women? I'll bet she
never forgets to nag you for money, eh, Itsik?"

Itsik felt the resentment rising within him—at his wife.
Why had Leah let him sleep so late? He made up his mind. As
soon as he walked in the door tonight he would give her a lecture she'd remember for a long, long time. . . .

Smoke

IN MY OPINION, the union of two people as man and wife is sanctified only when their ideal is to have children. Yes indeed!"

These words were uttered one day by Moyshe in the company of good friends, among whom was Chava. His simple but forceful statement etched itself deeply upon her heart because these were her sentiments exactly. And since, in addition, Moyshe was a handsome young man, she even remembered the tone in which he had spoken.

Afterward Chava repeated these words to herself numerous times, and whenever she did so, she could see the whole scene vividly.

They were all sitting around a table, Moyshe at the head, she opposite him, the rest of the people at the sides. They were speaking about their friends, close and distant, how they lived, how they had acted before their marriage and what had happened afterward.

When the conversation centered on the observation that many people wished to make their own lives comfortable at the expense of their children, and that this was considered "natural," Moyshe couldn't sit still. His sparkling black eyes darted feverishly around him, their pupils seeming to expand. His smooth, angular face was grave and more than a little flushed.

He spoke quickly, with considerable agitation, but with a peculiar kind of confidence in what he was saying. There seemed to be a struggle going on inside him, as if he were really trying to convince himself rather than the others present.

As soon as he finished speaking he lit his pipe, but he did it with such unusual rapidity that it was noticed by everyone. And not until he had taken a few puffs and let the thick smoke out of his mouth and nostrils did he seem to grow somewhat calmer.

For the rest of the evening the conversation stayed on the same subject, but Moyshe contributed nothing further. He sat silently, deep in his own thoughts. Whenever he disagreed with something he furiously struck a match and relit his pipe. A cloud of smoke floated before his eyes. And whenever Chava glanced his way she got the impression that he was far away somewhere, off in a gray fog. She recalled that when he stood up to leave, the others seemed to relax. His contrary mood oppressed them.

Only she alone appeared to understand what he had tried to say. She was truly sorry he was leaving. Without him, there was no longer anything of interest to her in that company.

He said good night to everyone individually. She pressed his hand tightly. As he did with hers.

Later, after Moyshe and Chava already considered themselves betrothed, she said to him once, "You know, Moyshe, that speech you made at the Twerskys that memorable evening—your views on family life—that was the key to my heart. . . ."

He looked at her fondly. "That's good. But I didn't say it to please you or anyone else. I said it because I believed it—and I still do."

"Did I accuse you of having ulterior motives? Why should that even occur to you?"

Chava was particularly irritated by his use of the phrase

"you or anyone else." He realized he had made a mistake and puffed ferociously at his pipe.

The first year of their life together everything went smoothly. They were the happiest couple in the world. He went out to work and she ran the household. Her home was always clean and bright. Every little corner sparkled and sang.

Every morning she sent him out with love and every evening she greeted him with joy. As she stood in the doorway, he could never leave her; she had to go back into the house first.

The only thing that sometimes worried Chava was: would she ever feel the sacred glow of motherhood?

But such moments were rare. They had only been married a year. Sometimes it takes two of three years. Besides, she had spun a beautiful secret about this in her heart, a secret that she had kept hidden even from Moyshe. When the time came and she felt the very first signs of that supreme happiness, she would not say anything to Moyshe about it. First she would get everything ready, and she would do it all alone, with her own hands. Not until later, much later, would she entrust her secret to her husband. And even then she would first demand a nice gift from him in exchange for her revelation. . . .

But then she felt a pang of regret for wronging him this way, even in her thoughts. It wasn't fair. Why should she keep the happy news all to herself? No. As soon as she was certain about it she would share the moment with Moyshe immediately.

However, because he never spoke with her about such things, because he seemed to be deliberately avoiding the subject, she felt offended and therefore soon forgave herself for her thoughts about keeping it a secret.

The great moment arrived.

One fine evening, going out to greet her husband, Chava was suddenly overwhelmed with the feeling that life was really beautiful, full of promise; life never betrayed those who hoped and believed.

Even the waves of homeward-bound, weary people, pushing their way like a flood through all the wide and narrow
streets, appeared to her to be happy. Even the huge, deformed
buildings, with their seven, eight and nine top-heavy floors,
now seemed to her straight and well constructed. At that moment she felt that there was no evil in the world; everything
sang and danced for joy.

Catching sight of Moyshe, her heart skipped. She did not
know what to do. Should she tell him of their new happiness
right then and there, or should she wait—perhaps at home
would be better—oh, how happy he would be!

"Hello!" she called, holding out her white, rested hand.
Her simple greeting overflowed with love and contentment.
So much motherliness resounded in her voice that many of
the passersby turned to gaze openly and appreciatively at this
lucky young woman who was so deeply in love.

Moyshe took her hand as usual and, for the last time,
they walked home happily together.

The table was set. The meal was more elaborate than
usual and Moyshe, noticing this, asked affectionately:

"What's the special occasion, Chavenyu? Why is tonight's
supper different from all the suppers of the rest of the year?"

She blushed, hesitated. But she immediately regained her
composure and, as if she didn't want anyone else to overhear,
she replied softly:

"Starting tomorrow, Moyshe, you'll have to earn more
money—I need to eat for two. . . ."

Her eyes filled with tears of joy. She ran from the table.

Moyshe stuffed tobacco into his pipe, lit up, took a long
pull and, blowing the smoke toward the ceiling, turned to his
wife:

"I've got to speak with you, Chava!"

She shuddered as though she had unexpectedly been splat-
tered with cold water. The tone in which he had uttered her
name frightened her:

"All right," she replied, her own voice dangerously close
to tears.

He spoke for a long time.

"Listen to me, Chava. Our children—I mean, the children that we—" He stumbled for a moment but soon righted himself. "The children that are born to us will not be like other children. . . ."

Her eyes opened wide with fear. She did not understand him.

"Our children must be given a good education. They must lack for nothing, so they can grow up to be generous people. Any sort of pettiness must be foreign to them. . . . Our children must serve as a model for others. . . . Therefore, Chavele, in my opinion, Chavele, we should not now—"

"What!" she exclaimed in alarm.

"Don't get so excited, sweetheart. After you've thought about what I'm saying you'll agree I'm right. . . ."

Chava sat there, a reproach frozen on her lips. She stared coldly at her husband. It seemed to her he was not speaking to her, that a stranger was telling her a terrible thing about someone else.

He puffed away at his pipe, emitting one mouthful of smoke after another. Silently he watched the gray clouds float upward, thin out, disappear.

Chava, sitting sideways on a chair, mechanially brushed a pile of crumbs back and forth on the table with a knife. Both she and Moyshe gave the impression of being earnestly engaged in some very important piece of work.

"Chava," he asked quietly, "is the bed made?"

His question made her suddenly aware of the deep wound in her heart. She felt a bitter hatred for the creature that was growing inside her. The sooner she got rid of it, the better. But she was immediately horrified by her own thought. Why blame the poor little baby?

In a tone of utter dejection she said: "A person would always be happy if he never accomplished what he strove for. . . ."

"And what is that apropos of, Chava?"

"Oh, the poor thing—he doesn't understand me!" she replied sarcastically.

Moyshe only shrugged.

She stood up. Her voice quivered as she recited:

"In my opinion, the union of two people as man and wife is sanctified only when their ideal is to have children. Yes indeed!"

Sobbing helplessly, she pointed to the bedroom. "Go, Moyshe, your bed is all made—"

Only now did he comprehend how terribly his words had hurt her. He knew it would be impossible to persuade her to give up the child.

So what had he accomplished? Causing her—and himself—so much anguish. He paced back and forth across the room, preceded and followed by a moving wall of smoke.

Chava collapsed into her chair. Looking sadly at the clouds of smoke pouring out of his mouth and filling up the room, she thought, "Smoke, it's all nothing but smoke. . . ."

Moyshe stopped at her side and said:

"Listen, Chava. I only wanted to ask your opinion—we'll do whatever you wish—whatever you say, silly. The child won't be in my way—on the contrary. I only meant—"

"No, my friend. Don't try so hard to convince yourself of something you don't believe. Everything is finished between us. I'll bring my child up myself. I'll be both mother and father. There are children in the world who grow up without any parents at all—"

The scalding tears rolled down her flaming cheeks one by one. Her heart was so constricted with pain that she could not weep aloud.

After a moment she stood up again, went into the bedroom, brought out a pillow and a blanket, and made a bed for herself on the sofa in the dining room.

Moyshe walked out of the room.

When Chava finally fell asleep she dreamed she had come into possession of a marvelous violin and that all unexpectedly the main string, the one which produces the tenderest, most heartfelt tones, had snapped.

She awoke. Sleep had fled.

In the morning, Moyshe did not go to work. He noticed that Chava was putting things into a suitcase. He was so distraught and disheartened, however, that he did not even know what to say to her.

When she left, he followed her to the door, but let her go. He watched her silently, his words stuck in his throat.

She did not turn around. Swallowing her tears, she walked and walked, thinking:

"Smoke, it was all nothing but smoke. . . ."

The Freethinker:
A Shtetl Atheist

LEYZER MANDEL the book-
keeper, or as he calls himself, Lazar Osipovich, gets up earlier
on Saturday mornings—when his office is closed—than on
the other days of the week.

When the worshippers are on their way to the synagogue
for the first *minyan*, Mandel stations himself at the gate outside his house. Summer and winter he stands there bare-
headed, holding his big, gnarled walking stick in one hand and
a cigarette in the other. Not that he smokes the cigarette
openly—that would be insensitive. He just carries it in such a
way that you'll know he is smoking, but you never actually
catch him puffing on it. Sometimes he turns his head to one
side, blows the smoke out of his mouth and looks around
with a smile of self-satisfaction.

When people pass by him without seeming to notice him,
without whispering to each other and pointing at him, he
starts worrying that the public has forgotten him. Yet it wasn't
too long ago that the whole town—as well as all the neighbor-
ing towns—had rocked with the news of his heretical behavior; now things have grown so quiet, it's almost as if people
are ignoring him out of spite.

Several times Mandel has resolved that one of these days, come what may, he must strike up a conversation with some of the more prominent congregants who pass by his house and find out what they are thinking, once and for all.

When the time comes to talk, however, he loses his tongue, doesn't know where to begin, or how, and the most he can do is utter a disdainful phrase or two about their piety.

One Shabbos morning he stayed at his post until people began gathering for the second *minyan*. As he was about to go back inside, he saw his close neighbor, Shneur-Ber, approaching. He waited. Now he would get to the bottom of it. With Shneur-Ber he would certainly not be at a loss for words.

He began rehearsing his opening greeting, because he didn't want the conversation to get off to a bad start. By the time Shneur-Ber reached him he had already practiced saying, "A pleasant good-Shabbos to you, Reb Shneur-Ber!" Yes, that would get his neighbor's attention. But as the man came closer, Leyzer became so flustered that instead of "A pleasant good-Shabbos to you, Reb Shneur-Ber," he said, "Reb Shneur-Ber, good-Shabbos!" He was mortified. That he, Lazar Osipovich, should make such an error!

Shneur-Ber did not even hear anyone talking to him, he was in such a hurry to get to the synagogue.

"Reb Shneur-Ber!" Mandel called after him. "You really didn't hear me, or you don't speak to freethinkers on Shabbos?" He stroked his goatee to emphasize the sarcasm in his tone.

Shneur-Ber, short and stocky, with a full black beard, and wearing a yellow cloth coat over his *tallis*, raised his friendly gray eyes and stopped in his tracks as if something were blocking his path.

"Are you speaking to me, Reb Leyzer?" he asked.

"Twice I said good-Shabbos to you and you refused to answer me."

"Refused to answer you?" Shneur-Ber exclaimed in real surprise. "How could you even think such a thing?"

"Never mind." (He stripped some peeling paint from the fence; let his neighbor see what he was doing.) "Anyway, where are you rushing to so early in the morning? To *shul?*"

"Of course! Where else would a Jew be going on Shabbos morning?"

"Why don't I ever see you going to the earlier *minyan*, Reb Shneur-Ber?"

Shneur-Ber began to stammer. "I—I—I like to read certain Psalms at home first, and by the time I'm finished, it's too late for the first *minyan*." Shneur-Ber was obviously discomfited; he wasn't sure this was such a commendable excuse.

Noting his confusion, Mandel pressed his advantage.

"I'll tell you something, Reb Shneur-Ber," he said with a knowing smile. "You're smarter than some of the others around here, so you know that early in the morning, God is still asleep and is not too happy with all that yammering coming from earth. But later in the day there's a better chance He will hear your prayers—at least He's awake. . . ."

Shneur-Ber smiled, too. "God *never* sleeps, Reb Leyzer! He's always wide awake. Ai, Reb Leyzer, will you never change?"

"Change? Why should I? You think I'm not enough of a *mentsh?*"

"That's not what I said, God forbid! You know very well what I mean! Well, good-Shabbos, Reb Leyzer. I've talked so much that I'll be late for services."

"Good-Shabbos, Reb Shneur-Ber! A good year to you!"

Mandel was upset with himself for having spent so much time with Shneur-Ber. It might lose him the respect of some of the others, talking so long with a man like Shneur-Ber. Was he worthy of so much attention from Lazar Osipovich? Who was Shneur-Ber, anyway? A long time ago, yes, he owned property and had a great deal of money. But his money was long gone and the bank had sold his houses. Even the presidency of the Bikur-Holim Society* had been taken away from him. Leyzer wondered what had possessed him to start a conversation with an ordinary man like that.

To calm his nerves, he went back into the house and began browsing through his bookcase. He took out a thick vol-

*Society to Visit the Sick

ume, leafed through its pages. It was a book he had started to read several times and always put down again. He could not imagine anyone reading all five hundred pages of such a tome. He closed the book lackadaisically and glanced at the title: *Dostoevsky's Collected Works.* A great writer, people said. Ah, if only he, Lazar Osipovich, could have written such a book! He returned it to the shelf and stepped over to a mirror. Brushing his hair back with his hand, first to the left and then to the right, he pondered which way would be more becoming if he were a famous writer like those who had written the books in his bookcase.

Lazar Osipovich lives a peaceful, contented life. For many years he has been employed in Lieberman's retail business and he is certain that no one there is more respected than he, even though some of the other clerks carry books around with them all the time and even read them in the office, something he would never do. But when it comes down to brass tacks, you can see they don't know very much. Because really, what can you learn from reading dozens of books one after the other? Each writer has his own views and doesn't hesitate to tell you what they are. But how can you possibly agree with all of them? It would drive him crazy.

Reading too much results in a kind of fantasy existence, anyway. A cultured man must read, of course. But not that way. These people who read all the time—do they understand the world any better than Lazar Osipovich does? You can ask any toddler in this town and he'll tell you that Lazar Osipovich is a highly educated person and a freethinker. As for his employer, there isn't the slightest doubt that he thinks more of Lazar than of those others who always have a book in their hands.

Yes, everything is fine, it would be perfect,if only they'd keep the office open on Saturdays. Then he would be the happiest man in the world. What a wonderful feeling it would be, just when the Jews are all on their way to *shul*, with their handkerchiefs tied around their necks and the fringes of their prayer shawls hanging down out of their long coats—and they

never walk, but fly, as though they will miss something mo-
mentous if they arrive a minute late—what a pleasure it
would be just at that hour to stroll to the office, swinging his
big walking stick, with all the time in the world. It wouldn't
bother him in the least to miss the prayers. And the entire
congregation would be ready to explode. . . .

True, even by merely staying home on Shabbos and not
going to *shul* he also proves the kind of man he is—but that's
certainly not all he has in mind!

When most of the worshippers are walking to the synagogue for the second *minyan*, Mandel gets busy with his
samovar, despite his wife's tearful objections. In the first
place, she complains, she is a God-fearing woman. Secondly,
what will people say? At least, if there was no Gentile maid in
their house to start the samovar on Shabbos, that might be another matter. But this way—

On the other hand, she knows it doesn't hurt him profes-
sionally; on the contrary, the more widespread his reputation
as a freethinker, the better. Nevertheless, she is afraid—especially, God forbid, for the children's sake. How often does it
happen in this world that children suffer for the sins of their
parents! Would to God it weren't so, but it happens more
often than not. . . .

Most of the time it doesn't trouble her that her husband
is known as a freethinker. On the contrary, one could almost
say it gives her pleasure, though she would never tell him so.
Whenever anyone bestows honors upon her because she is
Lazar Osipovich's wife, then she freely admits he is a freethinker, and well he should be; after all, he's not a tailor or a
shoemaker, but a man of refinement. Who else should be a
freethinker if not he? Still, she cannot make peace with the
idea completely and often remonstrates with him:

"So you're a freethinker, a cultured man. Good. Fine. Be
whatever you like, as far as the public is concerned. But what
about yourself? Deep in your own heart, don't you know there
is a God in this world, that you just can't go around doing
whatever you please, that He can punish you?"

Mandel listens, but says nothing. In his heart he admits his wife is correct: sooner or later God settles accounts. He resents her telling him so, however, because her constant reminders have forced him to start thinking about God . . . about death . . . and it depresses him. He tries to distract himself, to forget. But as if to spite him, her words keep floating back into his consciousness. "He" can *punish* you. The word looms large in his mind, in big black letters.

"You're a fool!" he blurts out, "a big fool! I'm just as religious as anyone else in this town!" He regrets the words even before they are out of his mouth. "What do you want of me? What do you think I am—a shoemaker? Or the bricklayer who fixed your oven? Go out and talk with other enlightened men and see whether their wives ever interfere in such matters! I'm not afraid of your God, but who asked you to lecture me? Better you should keep silent about such things. The less you say the better! You want me to show you what your God is? Here! Watch!"

He grabs the samovar and runs out into the yard. People are passing by. Some turn and stare at him curiously. His wife cowers in the doorway, frightened, motioning to him frantically to come back into the house. He pays no attention, but continues blowing mightily on the coals in the samovar.

Two of his more well-to-do neighbors stop to banter with the freethinker. Lazar is overjoyed. This is the opportunity he has been waiting for. Reb Zalman "threatens" to call his wife—she'll fix his feet. Lazar replies in kind:

"Reb Zalman, you can have my two *kedusha* prayers for ten gulden; believe me, they're worth much more. And you, Reb Nochem, can have my share of the world-to-come if you make me a reasonable offer!"

Reb Zalman calls to Leyzer's wife: "Taybl! Taybl! Come on out here!" For a while Taybl pretends not to hear. Finally she comes out into the yard. Small and slender, her features testify that she was once a very attractive young woman. Now, confronted by her neighbors, she blushes a fiery red, stands speechless, choking on her tears. Reb Zalman taunts her:

"Can't you stop your husband from doing all these foolish things?"

"Tell me, Reb Zalman, what shall I do with him? Tell me, and I'll do it. . . ."

Both neighbors sense such defeat in her tone that their hearts ache for her and they regret having started this whole "comedy" which they can't finish. Without even wishing her a good-Shabbos they turn and walk away.

His neighbors hardly ever speak to Lazar Osipovich. And of course, he never goes to visit with them, since generally he prefers not to associate with the "common folk." Even when he meets them every day on the street he never says good morning. Should someone greet him first, then, like any well brought-up person, he will respond, but haughtily, without even looking up. When all is said and done, are they his equals?

Therefore, on this particular Yom Kippur, when they saw him in the synagogue, they were filled with feelings of revenge. Aha—now they had him! But once inside the synagogue, he sat quietly, spoke with no one, kept his eyes fixed on the prayer book. From time to time he looked around to see if the congregation had taken notice of his correct behavior. Between services he was the first to go out to the courtyard. Many pairs of eyes followed him. All the congregants wanted to ask him the same question: All year round you laugh at us for going to synagogue, so why are you here today? But no one had the temerity.

Lazar understood very well what they were thinking, and it only made him more confident. Impatiently he strode back and forth across the courtyard, waiting for some daredevil to ask him the question. Oh, would he give him an explanation! He simply loves to explain things. But no one dared ask him anything—people know their place.

Finally, unable to contain himself any longer, he walked over to a circle of men engaged in earnest conversation. When they noticed him approaching, they made a place for him, knowing they were about to hear something memorable. He coughed once into his fist, as befits a person of refinement, reached for the handkerchief in his back pocket, and began his explanation.

"You must understand that for educated people there is no choice but to be freethinkers." His words had an immediate effect upon his listeners, who pressed closer to hear him better. Those who had just joined the group tried to learn what he had said. How sorry they were to have missed it! Lazar acted as if he didn't know what all the excitement was about. His voice grew firmer, louder, to overcome the buzzing in the crowd.

"As I have already explained"—the word seemed to explode from his lips—"it is only natural that we educated, cultured people, if we are to be true to ourselves, can follow no other course but to become freethinkers. But I ask you: What does that have to do with Yom Kippur? God is God—"

"And whiskey is whiskey!" someone laughed. The buzzing grew louder. Smiles of satisfaction appeared on everyone's face. Heads nodded agreeement.

"What else? Certainly! God is God! Who knows that better than we?"

They straggled back into the synagogue.

And Lazar Osipovich, the freethinker, is happy, too. Happy and contented. He had done his duty!

The Little Calf

Early summer.

On the hill where the Epsteins lived, narrow rivulets of water ran down, down, toward the bottom. Each rivulet found its own path, which it dug deep into the heart of the hill.

The flowing water babbled and frolicked with the children, who stuck their hands and feet into the soft, black, fragrant earth. They were busy with a very important task. They were trying to block the streams of water which ran rapidly down the hill, all the way down. They constructed dams: they piled up chips of wood, little stones, thick chunks of earth, hoping that eventually the dam would be strong enough to hold back the water.

And the child who was fortunate enough to accomplish this for a few seconds would wipe the black, sticky mud from his tired little hands and clap them gleefully.

Soon, however, the water would surge forward again and, breaking down the dam, would splash triumphantly over the children's faces.

Then their laughter would ring out so merrily and cheerfully that everything else grew quiet and listened to the sweet sounds of the children at play. Laughing along with the children was the big, black hill and its occasional patches of grass. Also laughing were the twisting, foaming streams and the silky cloudlets chasing each other swiftly around the sky overhead.

Suddenly a shadow appeared on the hill, moving closer and closer toward the children. Six-year-old Leo buried his hands deeper into the earth, in order to make sure he wouldn't slide down, and turned to face the approaching shadow. A smile appeared on his beautiful red lips as he recognized the shadow: it was only his sister Esther. But before he could tell the others that Esther was coming, she put her finger to her lips in a sign to say nothing.

Esther—twelve years old and slender as a reed—was running as fast as she could. Her hair came undone in the wind and slapped her face, now shining with inexpressible joy.

When Esther's shadow had stretched out over the whole side of the hill, she called out loudly and happily:

"Hey kids! Come here quick!"

The children buried their hands in the soft earth and lifted their happy little faces toward Esther.

In her great excitement Esther was unable to articulate what she wanted of them, but the children could tell she was eager to share some wonderful news with them. Finally, concentrating all her efforts, she called out:

"A baby calf! We have a baby calf!"

Overjoyed, eight-year-old Jake lost his balance and started sliding down the hill. He quickly stopped himself, however, but his clothing and his face were covered with mud. Crying, he climbed back up the hill, where everyone was waiting for him.

Now Esther was ready to report the news more calmly.

"A tiny calf, a little bit of a thing . . . yellow, with a white tail—yes, and half its face is also white . . . and it has long skinny legs and it says meh-meh—"

"Meh-meh—" all the children responded.

"Meh-meh—" the rivulets babbled, mimicking Esther and the children.

"Meh-meh—" everything roundabout laughed.

"Let's go see it!"

"Sh-sh—" Esther warned them. If they were quiet they could go to the barn and see the new calf.

Arriving at the proper stall, Esther opened the little door and peeked in. Assuring herself that Papa wasn't there, she stepped inside, intending to let the children in one at a time. but they were too impatient for that, and all pushed in at once. The stall smelled of springtime, of a newborn calf.

"Look! Look! Look at the baby calf!"

"Tiny little calf!" called six-year-old Leo, pursing his lips.

"Oh, how pretty!" echoed nine-year-old Henry.

The eyes of the children sparkled with tears of joy. They were so happy they didn't know what to do with themselves. Esther bent over and kissed the calf's muzzle. And the other children, as though they had just realized what they had to do, began kissing the calf so enthusiastically that they crawled over the divider and while they were at it, kissed the cow, too.

"Whose calf will it be?" asked eight-year-old Jake.

"Davey's, it will be Davey's," answered Leo, knowing that Papa and Mama gave Davey whatever he wanted because he was a sick boy.

Tears of envy filled Jake's eyes.

"Soon we'll all have our own calves!" Henry decided. "When Papa gets rich he'll buy a lot of cows and we'll each have our own calf!"

"Right! Right!" agreed Leo.

Esther picked him up and held him over the calf's back. The children, afraid she was going to sit Leo on the animal's back, began to scold her:

"No! No! He's too heavy for the baby calf!"

Leo clapped his hands ecstatically.

"Sh-sh! Somebody's coming, kids!"

The children ran out of the stall and skipped happily into the house.

"Don't say a word about this to anybody!" Esther cautioned them.

The children were in such good spirits that everything they looked at rejoiced with them. The shabby furniture shone festively. The slices of black bread and salty butter which their mother gave them tasted heavenly.

Mama and Papa exchanged knowing glances. Esther guessed that Papa was cautioning Mama not to say anything to the children about the calf, and somehow this knowledge frightened her. Her apprehension communicated itself to the children. Little Davey, knowing that he was privileged and could speak, tearfully begged his father to bring the calf into the house. Realizing that the children already knew about the calf, he agreed, but with one condition—that they didn't pester the animal, because in a few days it was going to a certain place where it would live until it grew up to be a cow. . . .

The children would have received this explanation without any suspicion whatsoever, had it not been for the sorrowful expression on Esther's face. Her father's words worried her so much that she could hardly keep from crying. The other children thereupon grew sad, too, but as soon as the calf was brought into the house, all their gloomy thoughts vanished.

A whole week passed, a week of sheer happiness. The children even forgot about their hill and its rivulets, as well as their friends in the village. They did not badger their mother for food, and whatever she gave them to eat was fine.

From early morning until late at night they were busy with the calf. Had they been allowed to do so, they would have slept with it, too. As it was, Leo took his naps alongside the calf, anyway.

One after the other, standing in line, they fed the calf from their own plates, as if it were a rare delight for them to share their last bite with this helpless little creature. Only Esther was not happy. Closely she watched her father's face, particularly his eyes, trying to discover whether the unthinkable was really about to happen.

And on Thursday, late at night, Esther heard someone carry out the calf, and then she heard conversation in back of the house between her father and another man. She strained to hear what they were saying, but could not make a word, so low were their voices.

When her father and the unknown man had walked a

little distance away from the house, Esther quietly got out of bed and, without a sound, tiptoed over to the window. As she looked out, she shuddered. Her worst fears were being realized. With her own eyes she saw the calf lying bound in a wagon, as her father and the butcher stood nearby whispering earnestly about something.

Her face grew hot and soon she felt tears rolling down her girlish cheeks. She watched at the window until the butcher rode out of the yard; then she crept back into bed, but could not fall asleep again. All she could do was think about the fate of the little calf—and cry.

In the morning, Papa and Mama told the children that in no time at all the calf would grow up to be a big cow and then it would give birth to a baby calf just as tiny as *it* is now.

The children had no choice but to comfort themselves with this hope, even though they somehow did not really believe it. Still, it was their own mother and father who had told them, so why should they doubt it? Maybe. Maybe.

That day they consoled themselves by telling one another how pretty the new calf would look.

But Friday evening, when the Sabbath dinner was served, and the meat was so unusually fresh and tender, Esther paled and could not put any of it into her mouth. Mama and Papa looked at each other in alarm. Esther burst out crying. The other children felt that something terrible was happening. Little Leo stared at his father and at Esther with wide-open, frightened eyes. Henry quietly left the table and went into another room. Jake and Davey wept bitterly. The meal went uneaten. Papa and Mama also left the table, avoiding the children's eyes.

The next day and the day after, the children did not go out to play on the hill. Sorrowfully they hung about the stall where the cow mournfully kept calling its calf. And each one of them shared her pain. . . .

A Simple Life

I   On THE DAY that Avrom-Chaim was supposed to leave home his parents quarreled heatedly. His father yelled and screamed at his mother, who sat silently, her tearful eyes downcast, and mechanically turned something around and around in her left hand. Then his father angrily marched over to the bookcase and took out a well-worn Bible. Leafing through it until he found the page he wanted, he handed the volume to the boy, pointed to a verse and ordered him to read it aloud.

Avrom-Chaim, to whom the passage was totally unfamiliar, stumbled over the Hebrew words.

"Say it aloud, my son," his father urged him on. "Say it so she can hear it! 'A house and riches are an inheritance from your parents, but a wise wife is a gift from God.' A gift from God, my son! You will have to pray to Him for many, many years before you are worthy of that gift!"

Avrom-Chaim barely understood what the words themselves meant or what his father was trying to tell him, but he sensed that his father was accusing his mother of something, his poor mother who now looked paler and more defeated than ever. His own eyes welled up with pity for her, and it took all his self-control to keep from bursting into tears. The incident moved him deeply, but he had no time now to think about it; he still had to say good-bye to his many friends, to boast that he was going away to learn a trade, that he was now practically a grown-up person.

In the evening, before the coach arrived, his father called Avrom-Chaim to his side. Encircling him with his knees, he laid both hands on the boy's shoulders and, looking directly into his eyes, said earnestly but now without tenderness:

"Listen to me, my son. You are going out into the world now to live among strangers, away from your parents. You will become a workingman, a *mentsh*. You must do your work diligently, pay attention to what the Master-tailor tells you, do whatever people ask you to do. Then everyone will love you."

Despite all his efforts, Avrom-Chaim could not help crying, but not out of fear. It was the first time he had ever heard such warm, simple words from his father, the first time he ever felt that his father really loved him.

His mother, however, could not bear to hear him cry. She wiped his eyes with her apron and stealthily—so his father wouldn't notice—kissed him on the forehead. Avrom-Chaim could see the tears in his mother's feverish eyes, deeply sunken though they were in their blue-black rings. When she held him close, he could feel the pounding of her heart, hear her labored breathing.

Later he heard her complaining quietly but insistently to his father: "In most families, when a child is leaving home, the father tries to comfort him. Here it's just the opposite!"

Her words had the desired effect. This time his father came over to Avrom-Chaim, pushed his little cap back on his head and said, in a voice even kinder and softer than before:

"There's no need to cry, my son. You're not going a hundred miles away from us. God willing, you'll come home for the holidays. Don't be afraid. Just remember the words I said to you before. Someday you'll find them useful. . . ."

2 Avrom-Chaim had thought that even though he was away from home, life wouldn't be so bad for him. But it didn't turn out that way. People treated him like an unwelcome stranger. He had to accustom himself to many unpleasantnesses, bur worst of all were the beatings. As a child he had always felt insulted whenever his teacher beat him; for a long time afterward he couldn't look the rebbe in the eye. But that was a different sort of emotion; it was much easier to bear. For one thing, he wasn't the only boy the teacher hit; once he got started, he punched several boys at a time. So that was quite different. For another thing, he had to admit that the rebbe was most always right. In this case, however, he believed that he himself was in the right, that he was being beaten for no reason at all, and besides, he was the only one being punished.

Very quickly he learned the difference between the Master's blows and those he received from other workers in the shop. Even when he was concentrating on a piece of work and from nowhere came a sudden, unexpected shove or punch, or when someone threw a spool of thread at him, he could tell without raising his eyes who the perpetrator was, and wondered what he had done to merit such attention.

Whenever he met an apprentice-boy from another workshop he would ask him whether he, too, was being subjected to the same kind of harassment. And if the other boy replied in the negative or even boasted that he was living an easy life, that no one ever yelled at him or scolded him, Avrom-Chaim would not respond or show any envy. He would only nod and say to himself, "Friend, you are not even a good liar. . . ."

Time dragged on, with all its hopes and fears. Holidays came and went and Avrom-Chaim had still not been home, simply because he had no money to pay the coachman. During all that time his mother, on her way to the doctor's, had visited him twice. On both occasions she had brought him cookies, clean underwear, and advice: he must stop being homesick, because there was really nothing in the shtetl for him to be homesick about; he would do better to concentrate on learning his trade as soon as possible, so he could become a *mentsh*. Then it would be better for all of them.

Avrom-Chaim therefore applied himself to his craft even more assiduously. Whenever the Master-tailor gave him a good piece of work to do he would recite the first chapter of Psalms to himself as he sewed—it was the only one he knew by heart—and pray to God to help him do it right.

The months passed. People stopped beating him. The Master even warned the other workers in the shop to stop annoying him, he was too valuable now for that kind of nonsense.

Avrom-Chaim still had a year and a half to serve before his apprenticeship was finished, and since he had not gone home even once, and had not lost any other time from his work, he would soon be earning money. The wages he would earn for the first three months he would send to his parents, and then he would make himself a suit of clothes and go home for a visit. These and similar childish dreams now filled his head.

But a few months before his three years were up, his father arrived looking sad and dejected. After a moment of small talk, his father handed him a *tefillin*-pouch and said in a trembling voice: "My son, it is time for your bar mitzvah. An orphan must begin to put on *tefillin* a year earlier than other boys."

His mother's death shattered him, tore apart all the golden threads his imagination had been spinning and left him feeling like a lonely child in a world of strangers. . . .

Little by little the better circumstances in which he was now living began to ease his hurt. His wound healed and soon he felt not pain but a deep respect and longing for his dead mother.

In the beginning he often thought about his father. Several times a year he sent him money. But when his father took another wife, Avrom-Chaim became so estranged that he stopped writing to him and began to think more about his own needs. Whenever anyone asked about his father, he would reply with a parable he had once heard from an old man:

When a father brings home a new mother for his children

it is like a loaf of bread that one cuts in half with a sharp knife; if you hold the two halves together you can hardly tell it was cut. But if you let go, it falls apart.

The listener would piously agree—yes, that's how it really is—and Avrom-Chaim would feel ashamed of himself, as if he had been caught committing a grievous sin. Quickly he would add: "But not . . . my father . . . honor thy father and mother. . . . May he live to be a hundred and twenty—I will say *kaddish* for him, of course." And then he would suddenly feel frightened. Why was he saying such terrible things? Was he not sinning just by talking this way?

In time, Avrom-Chaim became a "real mentsh," a breadwinner. He had earned everyone's respect. Matchmakers beat down his door. He himself thought he should get married. Since he was an only son, he had no worries about conscription into the army. In any case, he knew that it was one of God's commandments: a Jew should have a wife. What good would it do him to remain single? But there was a problem: he was afraid to rely on the promises of Gedalya or Sholem the matchmakers. Whenever they started touting their wares it fairly turned his stomach. Besides, he did not want to fall into one of their traps.

Once, while Gedalya was in the midst of one of his interminable descriptions of his clients' virtues, Avrom-Chaim summoned up all his courage and said:

"I'll tell you the truth, Reb Gedalya, I don't believe—"

"What!" the matchmaker exploded, his eyes blazing.

Avrom-Chaim became so frightened that he couldn't finish what he had started to say.

Gedalya continued at the top of his voice. "Can you show me one person who doesn't thank me for what I did for him?"

"You're telling a big lie," Avrom-Chaim wanted to say, but he only turned and walked away.

One day a woman—he knew her only as Zelda—stopped him in the street.

"My son, you want to listen to a foolish old woman for a few minutes? I knew your mother well, rest her soul. I know what a good person she was. Your father is a quiet, gentle

man. And you, my son, should also find a good Jewish daughter, not one of those flighty females who never do a stitch of
work and make their husbands' lives miserable."

Avrom-Chaim blushed, but he felt something reassuring
in the woman's simple, straightforward manner. He was glad
when she continued:

"If you wish, my son, I'll introduce you to this orphan girl
that I know. She has no clothes and no dowry, but she has
a mighty God, father of orphans, who will help her because
she has a kind and generous heart. I don't want any matchmaker's fee—not from you, not from her. I don't make a living pairing people up. But if God blesses you and you get married and things go well, you can buy me a pair of spectacles as
a present."

Avrom-Chaim's heart overflowed. He could barely restrain his tears. Had he not been so shy he would have kissed
the old woman right there in the middle of the street. He
wanted to say to her: "Zelda, I don't have a mother, as you
well know. Will you be my mother? I'll buy you your spectacles. I'll make you a relative and you can come and live with
us." But he could not get these words past his lips. All he
could do was whisper, so that she just about heard him, "Let's
hope so, let's hope so, from your mouth to God's ears!"

3   Avrom-Chaim lived very happily with his young wife
and thanked God every day for the gift. He found in her
an honest, unassuming woman and a loyal friend.

So he was delighted when his fellow workers in the shop
said to him one day: "Now, Avrom-Chaim, we'll at least have
a place where we can gather on Shabbos afternoons, if you and
Beyla can put up with us."

"Why not? Why not? What a question! You can come
every Shabbos! Every Shabbos!"

"And you won't mind if we sing Russian songs and take
off our hats?"

"Your sins won't be on my head," replied Avrom-Chaim
softly, although he wondered: perhaps the responsibility really
did lie with him, since he was in a position to forbid it?

"And what about heating up the samovar?" asked Leybele Ganef, winking one eye at the gang.

"Why should you do that? Better if I put up my big copper teakettle on the stove and keep it well covered—that way the water will be hot as a flame."

"Correct!" Leybele shouted, slapping one of his friends hard on the back. "You hear what he said? Every Shabbos afternoon we'll get together at Avrom-Chaim's. Now that's what I call living! What do you say, gang?"

So on the Sabbath, more than on any other day of the week, Avrom-Chaim felt that he was now a real householder, a *mentsh*, especially when he walked home from synagogue with the other *baalebatim*, his *tallis* on his shoulders and his handkerchief around his neck. For him it was a foretaste of Paradise. He loved very much to walk with the older men and was careful not to take longer steps than they did. He considered it an honor and wanted the whole world to notice. If only his mother had lived to see it! Even his father never had that pleasure. At times like this he thought a great deal about the topsy-turvy order of the world, where everything was just the opposite of what it should rightfully be.

Immediately after the Sabbath meal he would say to his wife: "Beyla, I'm going to lie down now for a little while on the fresh hay." This was his little joke about the cot that stood near the table, its embroidered spread depicting a grassy field with two haystacks.

"It's a silly thing," he explained to her once, "but whenever I lie down on this cot to rest, I get a funny feeling, the same kind of sad feeling that I remember from my childhood. When I was a little boy I used to feel this way every Shabbos at dusk."

"But why now? What is it you lack, God forbid?" This "funny feeling" of his always made her uneasy. "Thank God, you live in your own house, you're in good health, so what else do you want? Wealth? That depends on The One Above. If we deserve it, we'll have it, just wait and see. Or is there something else you're unhappy about? Tell me! Don't hide anything from me!"

"Go on, silly, what are you saying? Who's unhappy? What

is there for me to be unhappy about, God forbid? I'm just saying, it's a feeling that I remember from my childhood. . . ."

As he rested on the cot he would recall many inconse-
quential incidents of his youth. He knew they were trivial,
unimportant things, hardly appropriate for a mature, intelligent man to think about. But involuntarily—without his
understanding why—his thoughts went back to those golden
days and he found it pleasant to lie there and relive them. He
recalled, for example, how he and his friends used to scramble
up to the top of a grassy knoll, stretch out next to each other
and then, one after the other, roll down to the bottom. The
boy at the bottom of the hill had to catch those who rolled
down, otherwise he and the "roller" had to go back up, put
their arms around each other and roll down again. If you
could stand at the bottom of the hill and stop everyone without falling down yourself, you became The King. He had a
vivid memory of several of the kids rolling downhill, straight
into the stream at the bottom. He laughed out loud. Beyla
came running over.

"God be with you, what's wrong?"

"Nothing's wrong. Just something I was remembering."
He would have liked to describe the picture to her, but was
too embarrassed to tell her.

After his nap, when the other tailors gathered at his
home—along with two or three of Beyla's girlfriends—they
would all sit down around the table and he and Beyla would
serve tea and kugel. At such moments he would feel a sense of
exhilaration, though sometimes this mood was marred by the
indecorousness of the young men, with their Russian songs,
their bare heads, their suggestive language, and worst of all,
their conduct in the presence of the girls. Whenever anyone
uttered an improper word, Avrom-Chaim's face reddened, but
he pretended he hadn't heard it.

He would even the score, however, when old Yoineh arrived. It was practically a rule that Yoineh would visit him
every Shabbos afternoon for a special pot of tea. Avrom-
Chaim deemed it a privilege that Yoineh ate and drank in his
home while he told stories about the ways of the world and
about Jews in "the olden days."

As soon as Reb Yoineh came to the door the whole gang

would snap to attention and put on their hats—as well as their jackets, so the old man wouldn't notice they weren't wearing their ritual fringes. The girls, too, would make sure there was nothing "immodest" about their attire. All the young people had great respect for Reb Yoineh and did not wish to offend him.

"Good-Shabbos!" they greeted him.

"Don't mind me, children! Go right ahead with whatever you were reciting. Even when a non-Jew comes into a room where Jews are reading *Perek* or Psalms, it is permitted to continue—there's nothing to be ashamed of. On the contrary."

The "children" were a bit abashed by Reb Yoineh's words, because it was evident that he had heard them singing their songs and was deliberately teasing them.

Leybele Ganef, however, rose to the occasion. "Reb Yoineh, it so happens that we have a serious question to ask you. You taught us yourself that God wants Jews to be happy, isn't that so? Well, all week long we slave in the workshop. Shabbos is the only day of the week on which we can have a little innocent fun!"

"Of course I said that. And I say it again now," the old man replied, looking for a place to sit down. He had not even noticed that Avrom-Chaim was following him around with a chair.

"Please sit down, Reb Yoineh," Avrom-Chaim finally said respectfully.

Reb Yoineh sat down and continued the conversation. The rest of the company waited eagerly to see how the "debate" would go.

"Yes, children, I say the same thing today—God loves to see Jews happy. But tell me, can a Jew ever be happier than when he is serving God? All week long you are busy, you work such long hours. So if you can't observe the *mitzvos*, he will forgive you. But Shabbos and holidays—that's the only time poor people can have the pleasure of serving God properly!"

None of the young people except Avrom-Chaim and Beyla were pleased with Reb Yoineh's rejoinder. They exchanged embarrassed glances and winked at Leybel to speak up for them.

"Nevertheless, Reb Yoineh, we Jews don't take proper advantage of our holy days, may God not punish me for my words. The peasants now, that's when they really enjoy themselves—on their holidays! But not us! Why is that so?"

"Ha—ha! A good question, upon my word! A very good question! Why is it so? Because we're Jews, that's why!"

Reb Yoineh had won the point. Even the young people thought so. It was unanswerable. But Avrom-Chaim pondered a long time over the conflicting ideas that had been voiced here in his home. In his own way, he, too, wanted to discover the truth for himself.

4 Quietly and imperceptibly time rolled on, brushing aside whatever stood in its way. Twenty-five long, sometimes difficult, years had gone by since his wedding day. Beyla and Avrom-Chaim now had two grown children of their own. But it seemed to him that his life was following along an old, well-worn path. He still worked for someone else. The idea of becoming a master-tailor himself frightened and overwhelmed him. What would he do if there wasn't enough to go around for him and his workers? Also, he was older and not as strong as he used to be. Occasionally his eyes failed him. His joints creaked and his bushy beard rose and fell in time with his labored breathing. Because of that he no longer ate a midday meal.

In the evenings, when Beyla knew that it was time for Avrom-Chaim to leave the workshop, she would tie a clean apron around her waist and go out to meet him. She would much rather have changed her attire completely, but she was concerned lest her neighbors misinterpret her actions. What could it signify—going forth to meet her husband all dressed up—as if they had just been married yesterday! That was no way for settled people to behave.

If she went out to meet him and he happened to be walking with someone else, she would become flustered and offer some pretext for being out of the house—she was on her way to the store, or some other errand, and she would hand him the key because the door was locked!

Avrom-Chaim understood this behavior of hers very well

and was delighted with it. She could not fool him one bit, even if she *was* as smart as a man. "She has a good head on her shoulders," he would think to himself, but not once did he ever say anything to her about it.

When he came home from work at the end of the day, he would sit down by the window, or he would step outside, sit on the bench and look silently up at the sky. Lately he had grown more taciturn than ever. All he seemed able to think about was the order of the world, the order of the world. His greatest ambition was to find some sort of balustrade he could lean on as he walked the rest of the way toward the end. . . .

For this purpose he joined a Psalm Reading Society, a Talmud Study Society. He never let an opportunity go by to listen to a religious preacher, a lecturer, a Torah sage. And remarkably, the more he listened, the more he thought about what they had said, the colder and emptier he felt inside, as though the speakers, with their sermons, were removing something vital from his soul. He did not understand what was taking place within him. Ideas which never before would have entered his mind were now outlined in sharp focus as he thought about them continuously.

Day and night he wondered about the sun, the moon, the stars, the clouds, all the miraculous things in nature that surrounded him. He knew he was trying to wrest some sort of essence, some sort of secret from them. He regretted very much that he had not started on this quest earlier in his life. Had he done so when he was younger, who knows, maybe he would have learned something by now, explained something, understood something. So many years he had lived as a stranger in this world. Everything that was now so dear and important to him had been foreign to him then, and he hadn't even been aware of that.

Sometimes he wanted very much to be part of that wonderful sphere which he now only sensed intuitively without understanding it. He, too, wanted to float endlessly, like the clouds. It seemed to him sometimes that he heard a whispering in his ear:

"Soon, very soon, when your soul leaves your body, it will soar upward and become one with the sky, the sun, the stars."

And with a reverent fear, an awe-filled respect, he would lift his eyes to heaven.

Sabbath and holidays, when he had more time to rest, he would sit outdoors and his weary eyes would follow everything that happened in the sky. At twilight a gray melancholy would fill his soul, his innermost being, and he would feel pity for the dying day, for the setting sun, for himself. He was pained by a sense of loss for everything that was vanishing before his eyes, never to return.

He would bury his head in his hands and sit and think about the order of the world, and the silent shadows, braiding themselves into a solid mass, would steal up behind him and intone:

"Just as the sun flickers before it sets, so you, too, will meet your end, O son of man; like a candle, you will expire quietly. From the dust you came, to the dust you will return. The *why* of it you will never learn. . . ."

And he would awaken suddenly, as from a deep sleep, rub his old eyes with his withered hands, gaze for a long time at his fingers and try to imagine what they would look like when they returned to the dust.

"*Akh*, all is vanity!" he would think. For what have I lived and labored, toiled and struggled? To what purpose?

The life of a simple man—what is it worth?